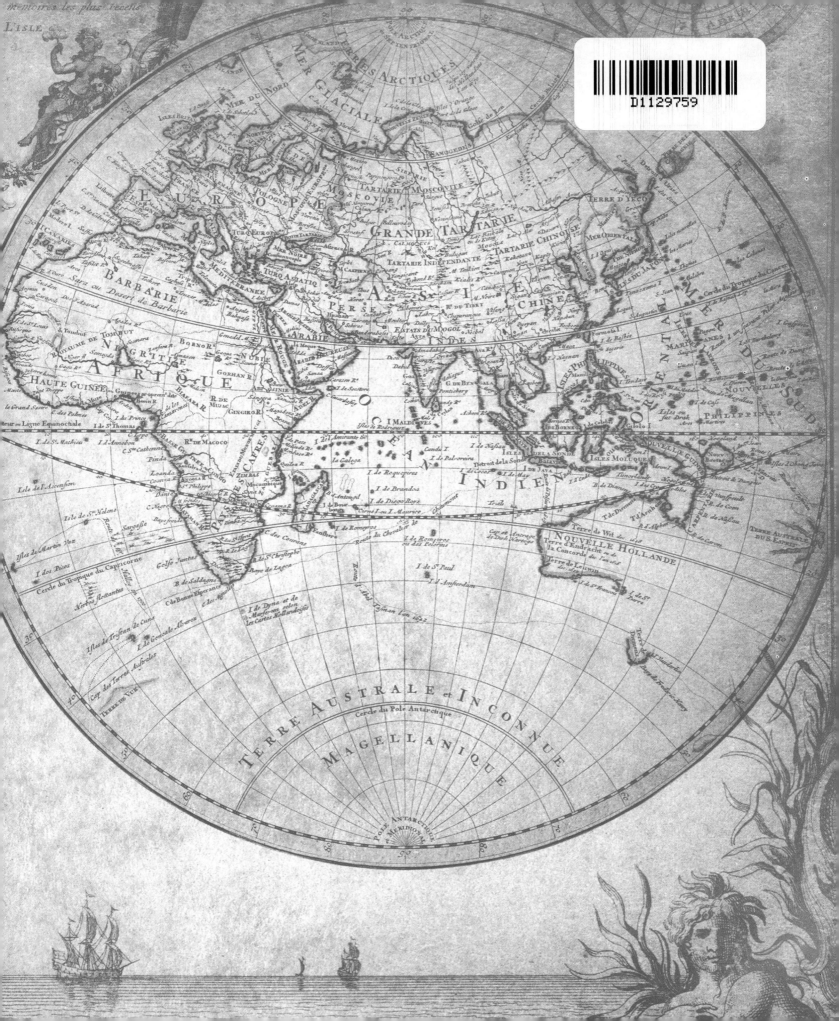

THE
STORY
OF
MAPS

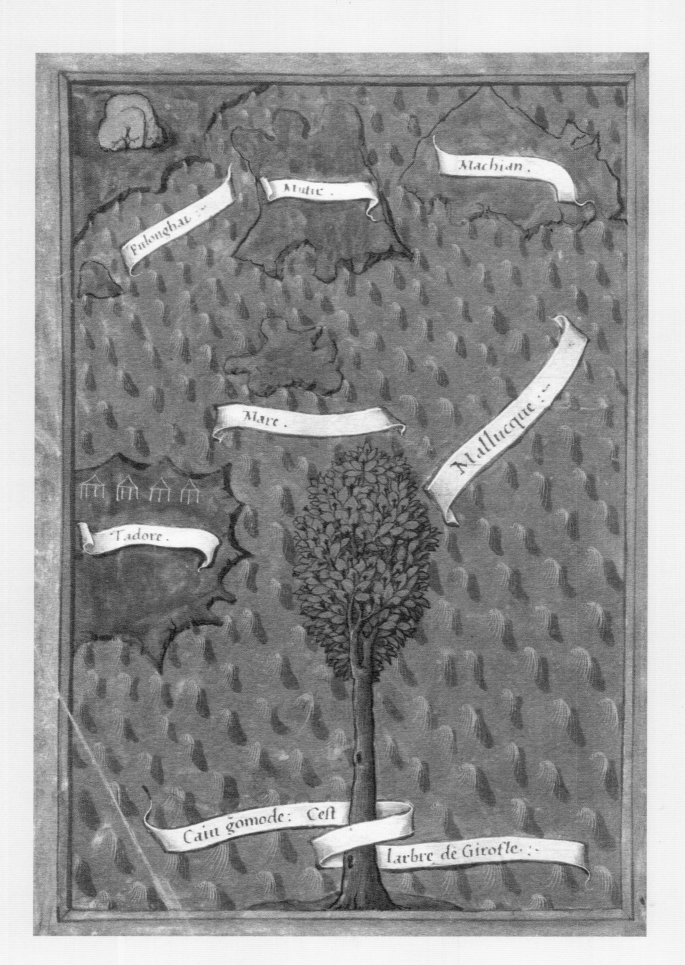

THE
STORY
OF
MAPS

PUTTING THE WORLD
IN PERSPECTIVE

ANNE ROONEY

ARCTURUS

Picture Credits

ARCTURUS

This edition published in 2015 by Arcturus Publishing Limited
26/27 Bickels Yard, 151–153 Bermondsey Street,
London SE1 3HA

ISBN: 978-1-78404-826-6
AD004457UK

Printed in China

CONTENTS

INTRODUCTION

'It is too absurd to say, that some men might have taken ship and traversed the whole wide ocean, and crossed from this side of the world to the other.'

St Augustine, *City of God*, 5th century

From the privileged position of being able to traverse the wide ocean in hours and see the whole world from space, it is difficult to reconstruct the experience of Augustine's contemporaries. Not only was the idea of crossing the ocean inconceivable, the shape of the land they inhabited was imperfectly known and there were, for sure, unknown lands beyond the borders that were home to unknown wonders.

The Story of Maps is the story of how humans have conceived of the world and their place in it. Any map uses conventions which its audience must understand in order to make sense of it. Our own mapping conventions are so familiar to us that we barely notice them. We only see them as a choice when exposed to those developed by other cultures, distant in time and often in place from our own. Why do we show the globe with North at the top when space has no 'up'? Why do we show Greenland as almost as big as Africa when it is actually only a fourteenth the size? Why do we depict individual buildings but rarely individual trees?

WHAT IS A MAP?

The Argentinian writer Jorge Luis Borges wrote a short story titled 'On Exactitude in Science' which concerns 'a Map of the Empire whose size was that of the Empire, and which coincided point for point with it'. In theory, this would be a perfect map, but of course it is not. For one thing, it is unusable. A map is not an exact copy of a landscape that, if enlarged, would be the same as the area it depicts. The conventions of representation which distinguish the map from the real thing don't just limit its mimetic function – they make it useful.

A map may be drawn to scale or it may not. The area may be shown from above, as though each landmark were observed from directly overhead (so suggesting infinite points of view), or it may be viewed obliquely as if from a high vantage point. If it is viewed from ground level, with buildings shown in elevation, we might ask whether it is really a map, which begs the question of what a map is, what we expect of it. As modern map-users, we expect to find a route or see the lie of the land. The map is often a guide to what we would find if we visited the area. But it has not always been so. The Aztecs made maps that showed a highly stylized image of the landscape, but included their cultural history (see page 35). The Marshall Islanders made maps from sticks and shells that recorded the currents important to navigators, but did not show what any area looked like (see page 184). The map-makers of the European Middle Ages were more concerned with recording the spiritual geography and history of the world than with topography.

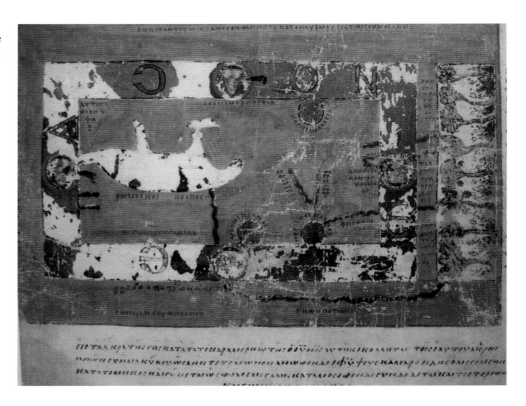

A map of the known world in Augustine's day by Cosmas Indicopleustes, c.550. The rectangular world is surrounded by an ocean that is connected to the Mediterranean Sea.

Mapa de Cuauhtinchan no.2 is a 16th-century Mesoamerican cartographic history from Cuauhtinchan, to the east of the valley of Mexico. It shows a ritual pilgrimage made by the leaders Icxicohuatl and Quetzaltehueyac between Cholula and the mythical Chicomoztoc, 'The Place of the Seven Caves'. The Aztecs and other peoples of Central Mexico were believed to have emerged from Chicomoztoc, which is illustrated along with other important sites and events.

WHY MAKE MAPS?

Maps can be made and used to find your way or show a route to others; to record land ownership or discovery; as an aid to industries such as farming and mining; or as a political tool. Today, we class all these diverse uses together, but neither the pre-Islamic Arab languages nor the medieval European languages had a single word for 'map', suggesting that those people saw no continuity between the functions of these different types of representation of the land and sea.

However much they might claim to, maps never really show a 'true' representation of the world. The very act of representing the surface of a sphere on a flat map necessitates distortion.

The quest for 'truth' can itself be used as a political tool. The map drawn by Michael Lok (see page 8) in 1582 gives a simplified view of North America, missing out the northwest part of Canada, which was known. The gap made access to the Pacific appear easier than it is. Lok's purpose was to encourage investment in exploration, in seeking a northwest

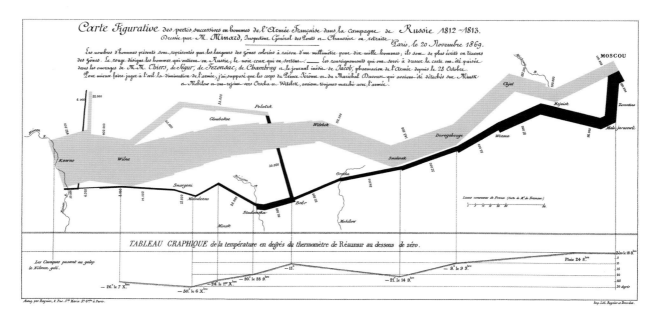

Charles Joseph Minard's map/graph of Napoleon's retreat from Moscow shows the route taken by the troops (brown to Moscow, black for the return journey). The thickness of the line indicates the number of troops surviving at any point.

As well as missing out part of Canada, Michael Lok reduced the size of Meta Incognita (a peninsula on the south of Baffin Island) and increased the size of Lok, an island named after him.

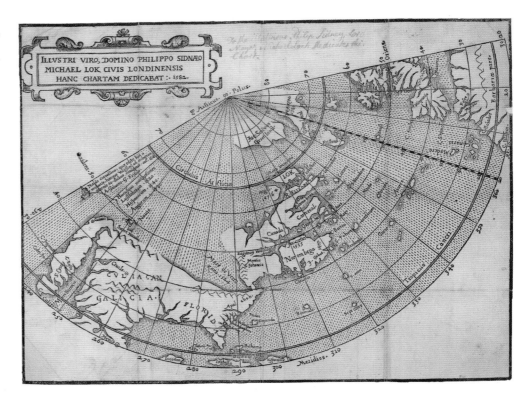

passage, and in colonizing part of North America. In 1490, Henricus Martellus extended the south of Africa (see pages 140–1), possibly with the intention of promoting Columbus's case for sailing west (by making the trip around Africa look longer than it is). Perhaps the most audacious example of exploitation is found in the world map of Diogo Ribeiro in 1529: he drew the Spice Islands (Moluccas) on the Spanish side of an agreed line that divided the Pacific between Spain and Portugal. In fact, the Moluccas are on the Portuguese side of the line, but Ribeiro's map was accepted and the islands became a Spanish territory. The deception was not discovered for several centuries.

Whether or not they intend to, maps also record a moment in time. The map of the changing path of the Mississippi river on page 186 is a reminder of the impermanence of our landscape. It's easy to think that the world mapped by our ancestors was the same world we inhabit now, but things change. Early maps of East Anglia show Ely as an island, with much of the fenland under water. Maps drawn before and after volcanic eruptions show islands and the atolls they have become.

HOW WE MAKE MAPS

The earliest maps show the land people saw around them. The depiction of the world outside their immediate vicinity relied on travellers' tales, mythology and guesswork. Measurement was the first tool to be employed in mapping, and the first attempt at measuring the Earth was made by the Ancient Greek Eratosthenes around 200 BC. It was Eratosthenes, too, who first developed longitude and latitude as a system for specifying points on the globe.

Surveying techniques with simple ropes and weights were known to the ancients and used in Egypt by 2700 BC. The Romans had professional surveyors; the ambitious Tabula Peutingeriana (pages 66–7) maps over 100,000 km (65,000 miles) of roads around the Roman Empire. Triangulation, a method of mapping an area in measured triangles, was introduced in 1615 by the Dutch mathematician Willebrord Snellius. This made possible the great national mapping projects, starting with Cassini's map of France (pages 50–1). The development of the theodolite in the 18th century saw a further revolution in inland map-making. It allowed measurement of angles in vertical and horizontal planes, enabling altitude to be mapped. The Great Trigonometric Survey of India, begun in 1801, first mapped and named Mount Everest.

At sea, mapping and measurement present very different challenges. There are no points of reference from which accurate measurements can be made, and the curvature of the Earth plays havoc with measuring long distances and directions. Latitude is fairly easy to determine from the position of the sun at noon and a reference table, but longitude requires reference points for measurement. The inability to navigate accurately on long sea voyages led to frequent tragedies and the determination of longitude became an urgent problem, with various solutions proposed and tried between the 17th and 19th centuries.

Francesco Rosselli's map, produced in 1508, was one of the first printed maps to show the New World, though suggesting – as Columbus believed – that it was connected to Asia. It also shows a hypothetical southern landmass long before Antarctica was discovered. The map uses a new, oval projection which was adopted by many of the great map-makers of the 16th century.

THE LOST MAPS

Many maps have been ephemeral, lasting only a few days or even minutes. We know of some of these. The Maori drew on the decks of Captain Cook's ship with charcoal, and aboriginal Australians drew maps in sand and soil. Of enduring maps, there are records of some that have been lost. The earliest known world map from Ancient Greece, drawn or described by Anaximander (c.611–546 BC), put the Aegean Sea near the centre. The lands above and below the Mediterranean were included, a relatively narrow strip considered to be the habitable world, including Greece, Italy and Spain to the north and Libya and Egypt to the south. Palestine, Assyria, Persia and Arabia were to the east of the sea. Further north Anaximander considered too cold and further south too hot to be habitable. The enduring legacy of Classical mapping was Claudius Ptolemy's 2nd century model of the world, divided into seven 'climates' (bands of latitude) of which, as in Anaximander's model, only the middle bands were habitable. Although he may never have drawn a map, Ptolemy's description in his *Geographia* formed the basis of much later mapping, still centred on the Mediterranean, using longitude and latitude to specify precise locations. His model was used for more than a thousand years in Europe, being adapted to incorporate new discoveries. Martin Waldseemüller's *Universalis Cosmographia* (pages 150–1), published in 1507, puts a portrait of Ptolemy over the Old World and Amerigo Vespucci over the New World.

Many millions of historic maps survive, but many more have been lost. Maps could be for display or use. Those for use were frequently damaged, destroyed, lost or thrown away when superseded. Those for display were more likely to survive, but often replaced when they were no longer considered accurate.

The selection here brings together maps that were of singular importance in their own right, with some that are representative of types of maps and a few that are intriguing oddities. We can only wonder at the lost maps in the gaps.

CHAPTER 1

THIS LAND IS OUR LAND

Inevitably, the earliest maps were of local areas – the landscape and settlements inhabited by the map-maker.

THE URGE TO DEPICT our surroundings, whether for purposes of navigation or to record land ownership, goes back thousands of years. Some of the earliest artifacts that might be maps are difficult to confirm: are they sinuous or geometric patterns, or representations of rivers, hills and dwellings? Later, people drew, inscribed or carved plans of their settlements and cities, the local rivers and coasts they navigated, and sites that had special spiritual significance for them. From the 16th century, civic pride was a spur to map-making in Europe, with detailed city plans celebrating the power and prestige of new and old urban centres. And from the 18th century, with the advent of new techniques of surveying and measuring, the local map took on a larger scale, with the first of the great national mapping projects.

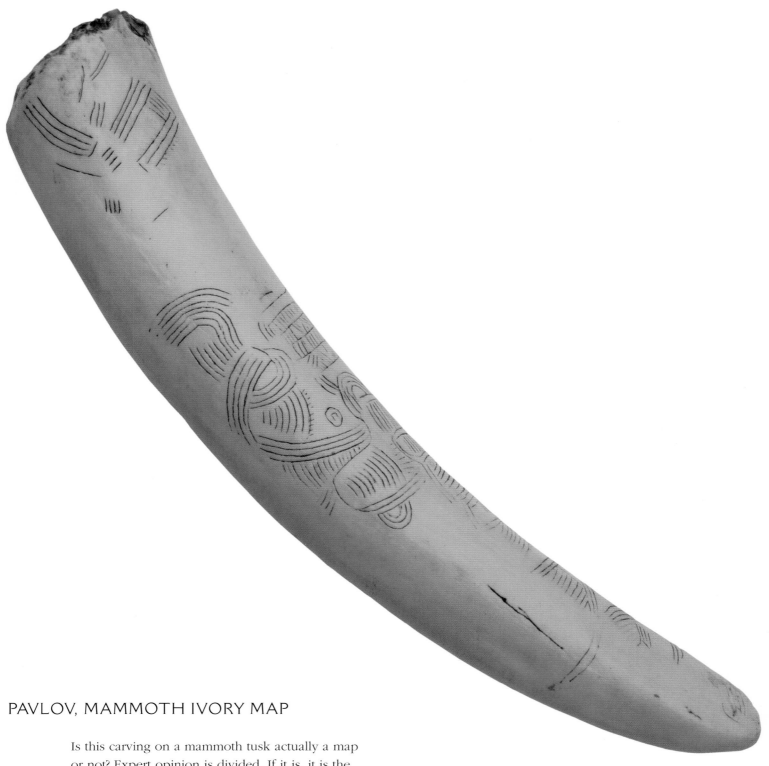

PAVLOV, MAMMOTH IVORY MAP

Is this carving on a mammoth tusk actually a map or not? Expert opinion is divided. If it is, it is the oldest map in existence, dating from Palaeolithic times. It was made around 25,000 years ago near the area that is now Pavlov in the Czech Republic. Those who argue that it is a map say it shows the meandering Dyje river and the rocky peaks of the Pavlovske hills. The ridges and eroded gullies of the slopes are also clear. A motif of a circle with a half-circle is interpreted as the settlement or home of the artist. It's said to match the landscape formation of the area where it was found, looking towards the south.

THE BEDOLINA MAP

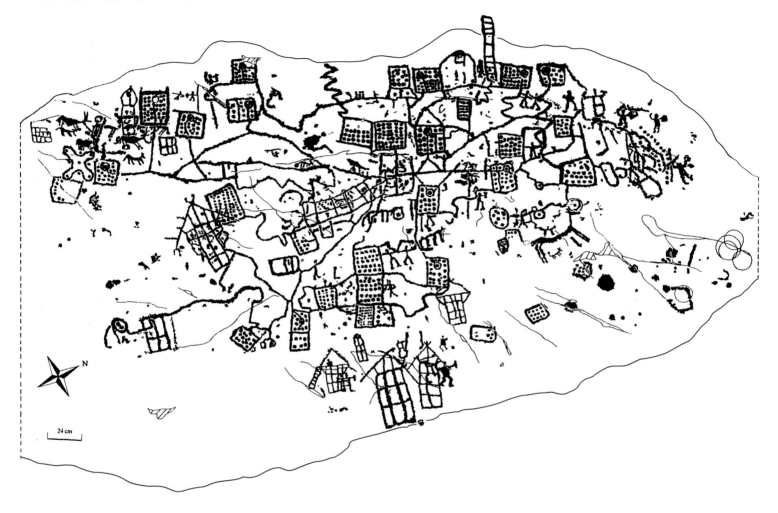

24 cm

The Bedolina map in Val Camonica, Brescia, Italy, is part of a huge field of up to 300,000 petroglyphs (images drawn or cut into stone). Begun in Palaeolithic times and carved over 8,000 years, the petroglyphs perhaps represent the longest-running public art project. Serious activity at the site ended during the 1st millennium BC under the Iron Age Camuni people. The petroglyphs considered to represent a map, on Rock 1, were probably carved in the 4th–6th centuries BC. The map shows zigzagging paths, six huts or houses, 30 fields, human figures, animals and a ladder. Some of the fields contain a circular element, which might represent either a dwelling or an enclosure for animals.

The tracing of the Bedolina map, above, shows First Iron Age warriors overlain with engravings of Late Iron Age huts.

NIPPUR – TOWN PLAN

This fragment of a map of Nippur in Babylon might be the oldest surviving town plan drawn to scale. It has been cut into a clay tablet, the typical writing medium of the culture. Dating from around 1500 BC, it shows the principal Babylonian temple of Enlil in its enclosure (on the right edge of the map); the city walls with seven gates; the River Euphrates; canals, storehouses and a park (to the left). Names and distances are marked in the Babylonian cuneiform script. Excavations of the remains of Nippur have not yet established whether the plan is drawn to an accurate scale.

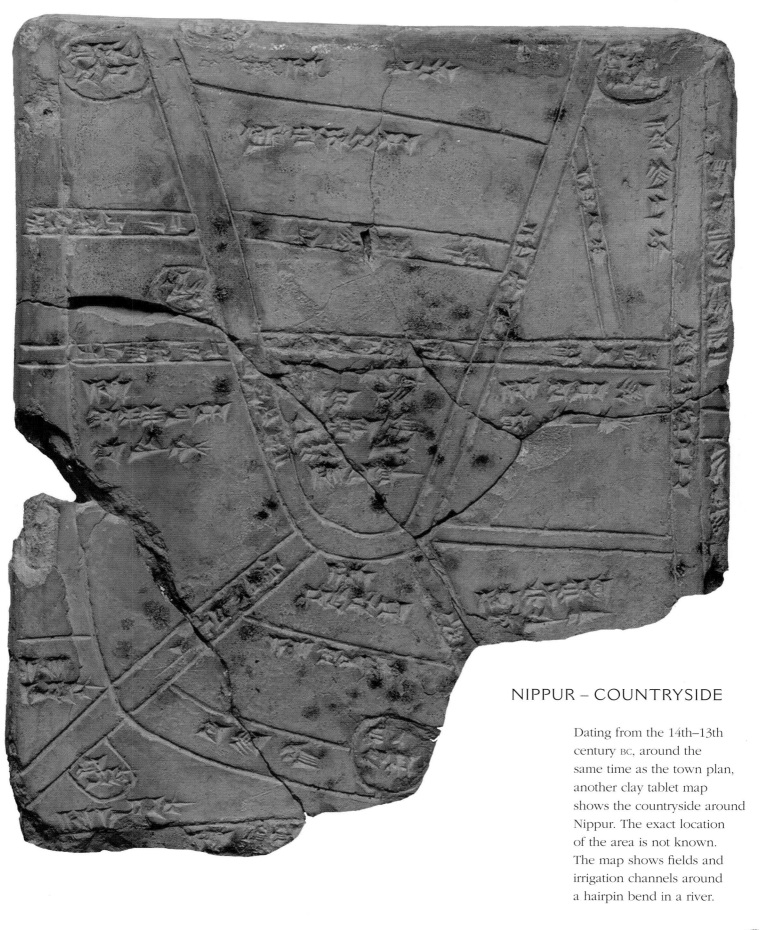

NIPPUR – COUNTRYSIDE

Dating from the 14th–13th century BC, around the same time as the town plan, another clay tablet map shows the countryside around Nippur. The exact location of the area is not known. The map shows fields and irrigation channels around a hairpin bend in a river.

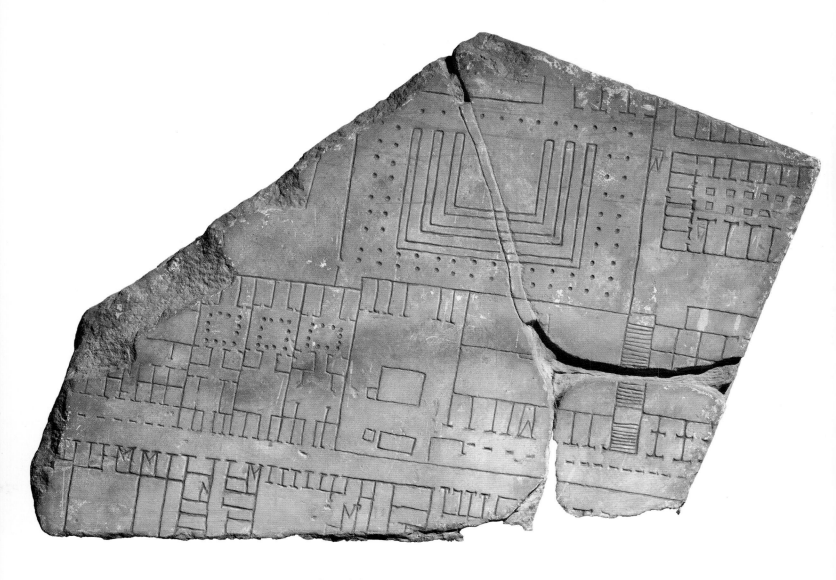

FORMA URBIS ROMAE

The once-vast Forma Urbis Romae was an engraved marble plan of the city of Rome, 18.3 m (60 ft) wide by 13 m (42½ ft) high, probably made between AD 203 and 208. It was originally fixed to the outer wall of the library of Vespasian's Temple of Peace in Rome. The average scale is 1:240 or 1:250, but important buildings are drawn at a larger scale. Although most of the city is shown in plan view, some features are drawn as elevations, including the arches supporting aqueducts. It would be another 1,500 years before an equally accurate plan of Rome was drawn.

MAWANGDUI SILK MAP

This map is one of three found in a tomb at Mawangdui in Hunan province, China. They date from 168 BC at the latest. The topographical map shown here represents an area in the southern part of Changsha state, showing rivers and mountains. It is drawn using vegetable colours on silk. All three maps are planimetric – they show the landscape in plan form from above. South is at the top.

MADABA MOSAIC

A mosaic floor in the Church of St George at Madaba, Jordan, shows the earliest surviving representation of the Holy Land. It is the most important example of Byzantine cartography, and the earliest image of Palestine. The map was used to educate the congregation, and is annotated with information from the Bible about various locations. The Mediterranean coast is artificially straightened, distorting directions.

Made AD 542–70, the mosaic was originally 24 m x 6 m (79 ft x 20 ft) and possibly showed the area from Byblos and Damascus to Mount Sinai and Thebes in Egypt. The fragment remaining is 10.5 m x 5 m (34.5 ft x 16.5 ft). The scale varies between 1:15,000 in central Judea to 1:1,600 in Jerusalem, the city being shown disproportionately large because of its importance.

MAP OF THE NILE, AL-KHWÂRIZMI

Al-Khwârizmi (780–850) compiled a manuscript catalogue of notable places, such as towns, mountains, rivers and springs listed by climate (following Ptolemy's division of the habitable world into seven 'climates', arranged as bands of latitude). The climate bands are vertical here because of the orientation of the map, with east at the top. This map is one of four from a manuscript copy made around 1000–1050; it's not known whether the maps originated with al-Khwârizmi or were added later. They are the earliest surviving maps from the Islamic world. The Nile is shown rising on the right as two groups of streams in the mythical Mountains of the Moon and disgorging into the Mediterranean at Alexandria on the left.

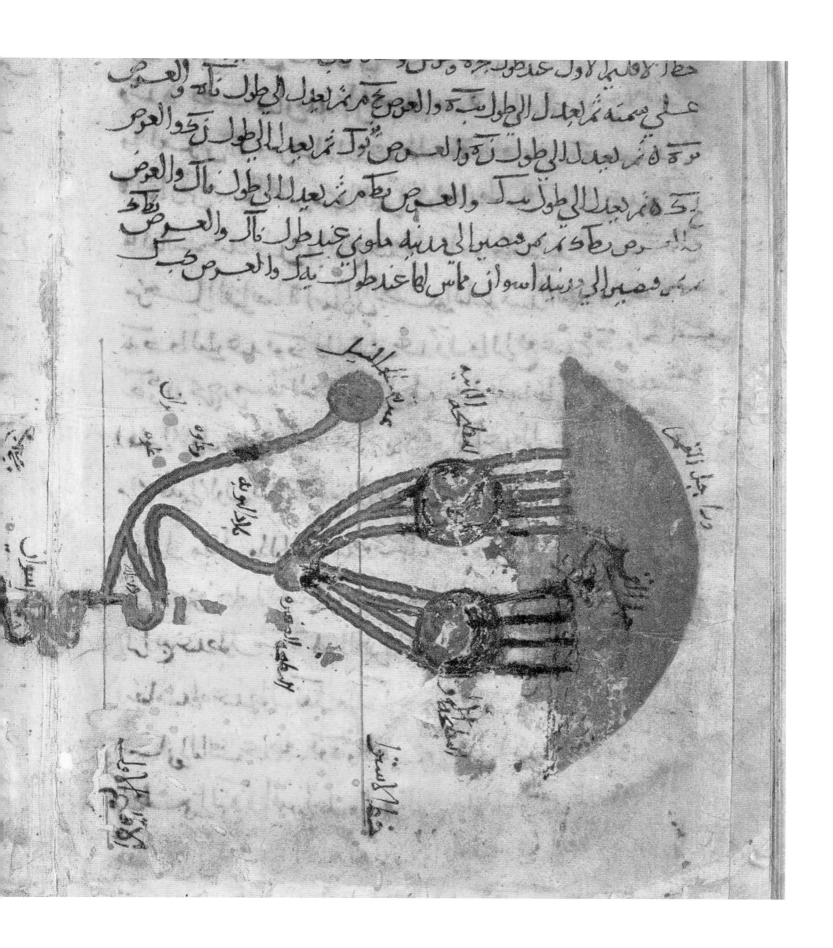

Maps of the Islamic Balkhi school look more like beautiful abstract images than cartography. This map of southern Russia and Azerbaijan is part of a collection sometimes called the 'Islam-atlas' and was drawn by al-Istakhri in 952. The collection illustrates geographical texts, and comprises a world map, maps of three seas (the Mediterranean, the Indian Ocean and the Caspian Sea), and 17 areas of the Islamic world. They cannot be placed together, like tiles, to produce a continuous map, but show discrete areas of the world known to the Abbasid caliphate in the 10th century.

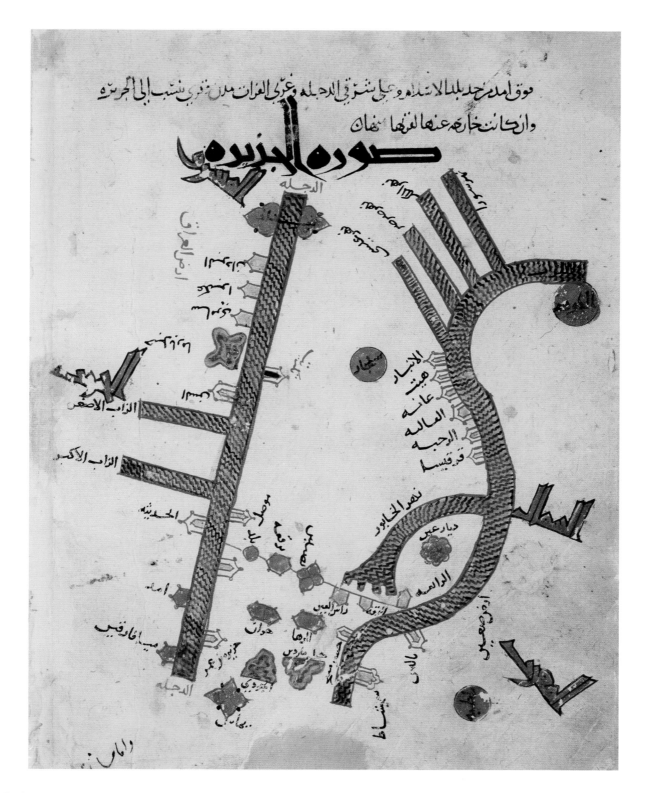

TIGRIS AND EUPHRATES, AL-ISTAKHRI

Another map by al-Istakhri shows the rivers Tigris and Euphrates that form the boundaries of Mesopotamia. All features in maps of the Balkhi school are drawn as straight lines or simple curves. Rivers are broad bands of blue with parallel sides. Features including lakes and towns are drawn as regular geometric shapes such as circles, squares and four-pointed stars. There is no concept of scale, but the maps show distances as travelling times between stopping posts. The point of the maps seems to have been to show the caravan routes with their stages.

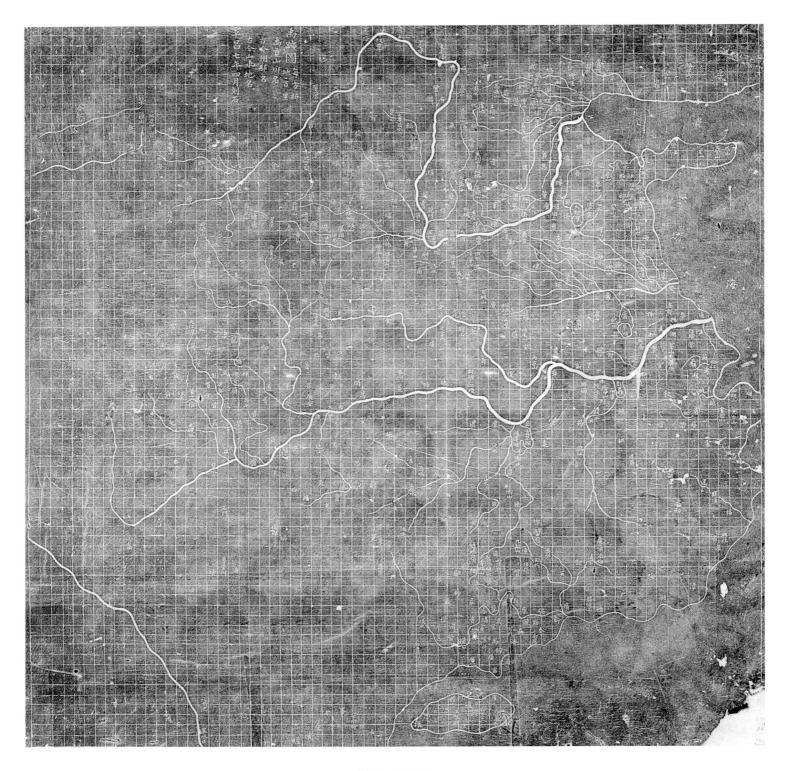

高麗圖地百折
烏古山川名里
古州郡名
今名小地名
旱昌七年四月刻石

YU JI TU

A map carved onto a stone stele a metre tall in 1137 shows the Chinese coastline and the network of rivers, particularly the Yangtze and the Yellow River, with great accuracy. It is called Yu ji tu or 'the tracks of Yu', referring to a legendary text called *Gong Yu*. Drawn onto a grid of 5,000 squares, it is the earliest Chinese map to use a grid. Each square represents one *li* (about 50 km / 32 miles). The map shows an ancient, unified China – though China was far from unified during the Song Dynasty when the map was made. As a stele, the stone also worked as a printing block and could be used to make paper maps by first inking the stele and then pressing paper against it.

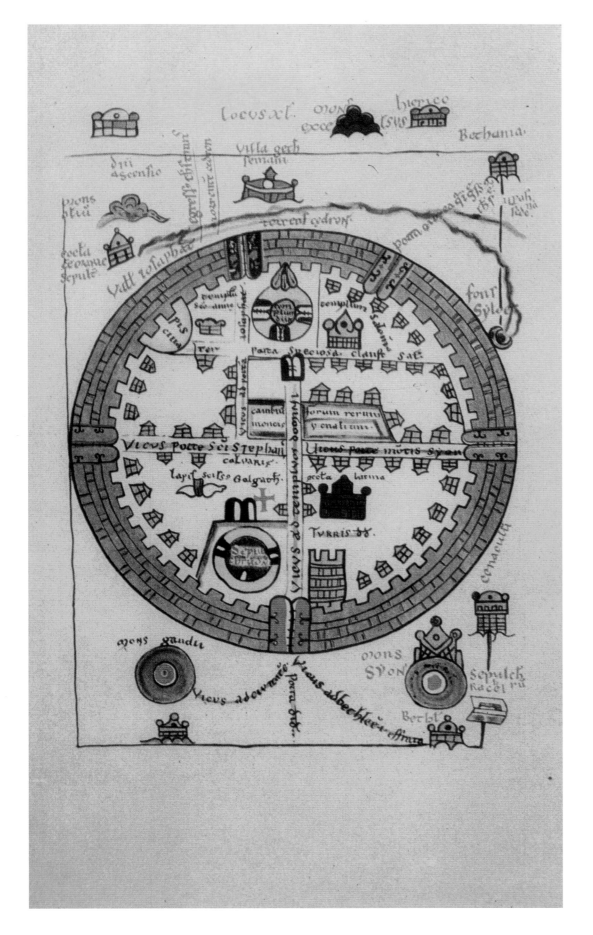

ST OMER CRUSADER MAP OF JERUSALEM

Maps of Jerusalem and the Holy Land formed the first tradition of city maps in Europe, beginning soon after the seizure of Jerusalem by the Crusaders in 1099 and the foundation of the crusader states. The early maps, such as this crusader map drawn in the 13th century, conventionally show the city as circular, surrounded by the city wall with its gates, and the principal roads. Buildings within the city are drawn in elevation. Roads and buildings not of interest to pilgrims or crusaders are not shown, so a lot of the area within Jerusalem is left blank.

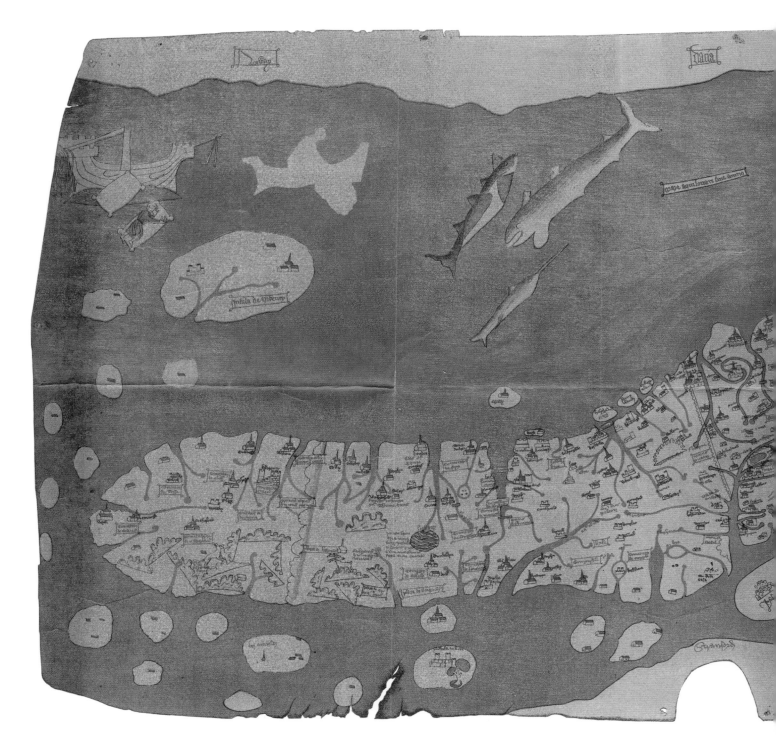

THE GOUGH MAP OF BRITAIN

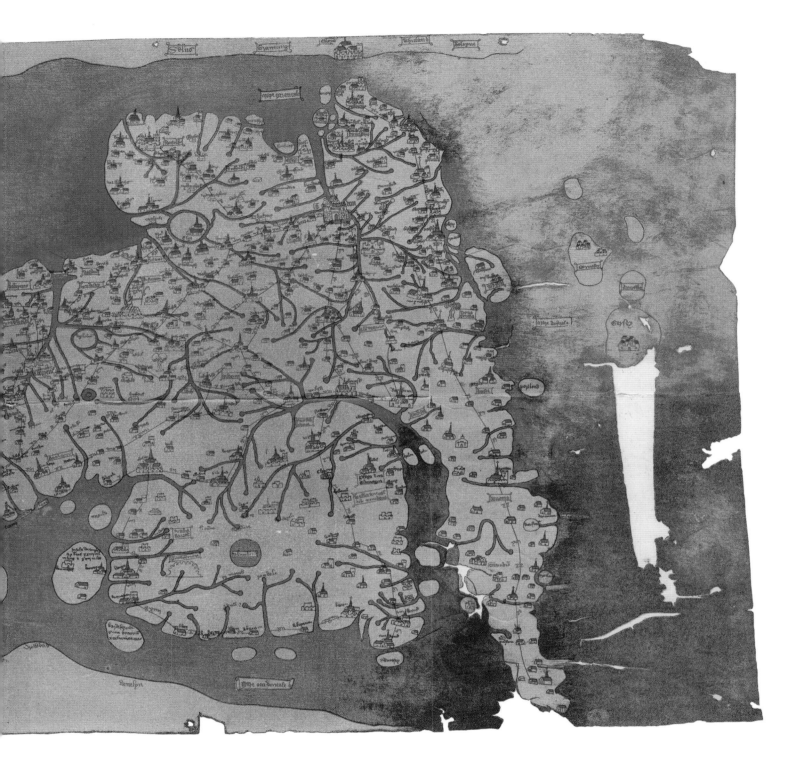

The Gough map is the earliest surviving roughly accurate map of Britain, drawn 1355–66. It is related to the itinerary maps (see Chapter 2) in that its details are clustered around five main arterial routes from London. It shows rivers, towns and coastline outside these routes, and some local roads in Yorkshire and Lincolnshire. Its proportions are broadly accurate, though less so – and the shape of the coastline less accurate – in Wales, Cornwall and Scotland. It is not, though, properly drawn to scale. Distances between places are marked along routes, using the variable local miles, but the distances marked don't correspond directly to distances on the map. East is at the top.

ALBERTINISCHER PLAN

This map of Vienna and Bratislava, known as the Albertinischer plan, is the earliest known local map of part of Europe drawn properly to scale, and the earliest map of Vienna. It follows the most common convention for representing towns and cities, and one found in many ages and cultures: it shows the city wall in bird's-eye view, and then the towers or gates in the wall and the buildings inside the city as elevations. The scale, graduated in paces, is shown in the scale bar at the bottom right. The surviving map is a mid-15th century copy of an original drawn in 1421–2.

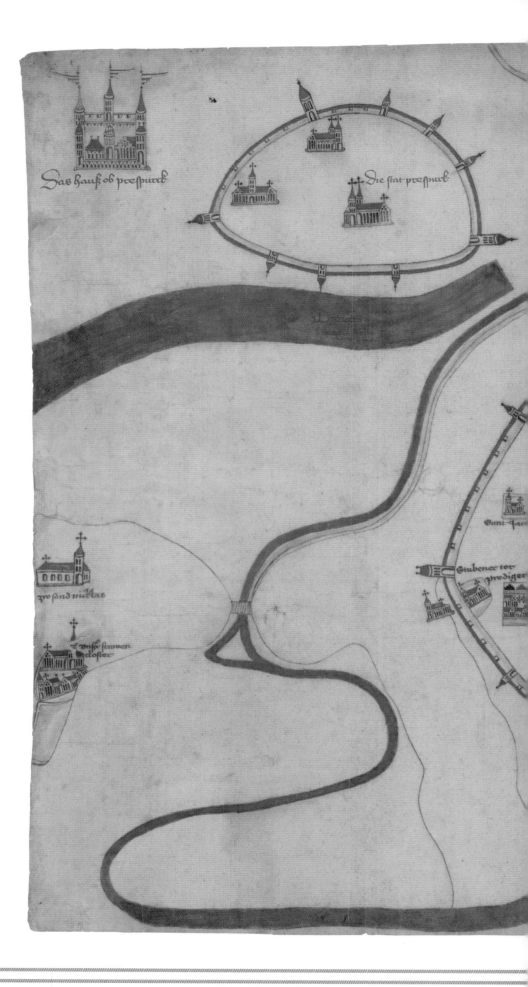

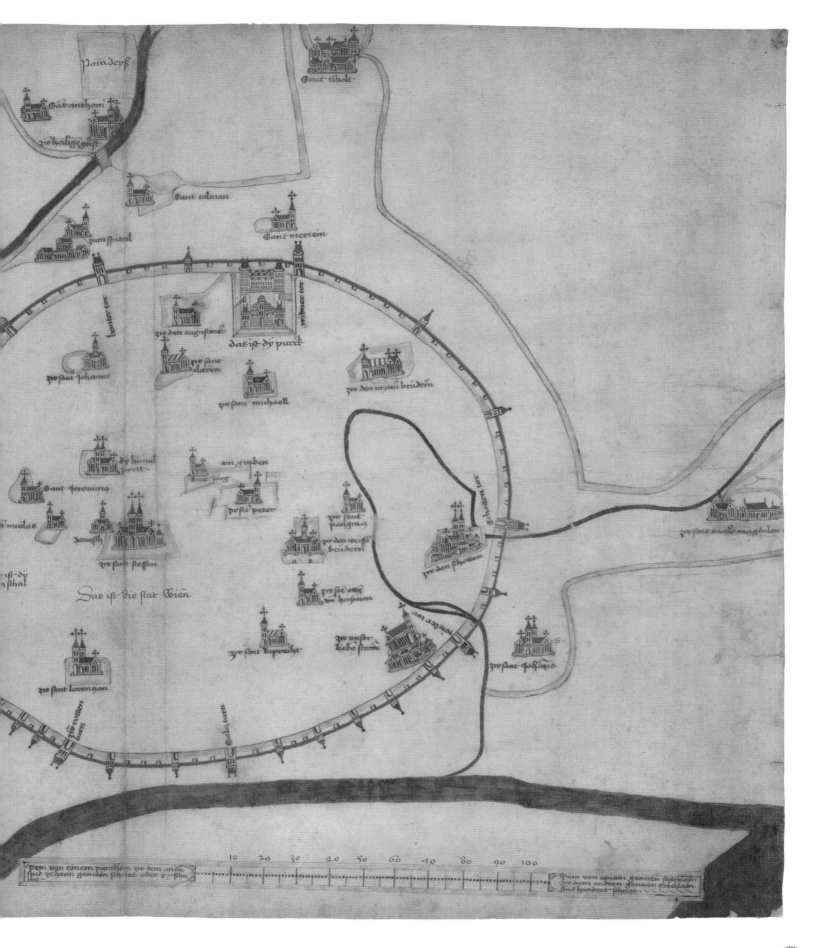

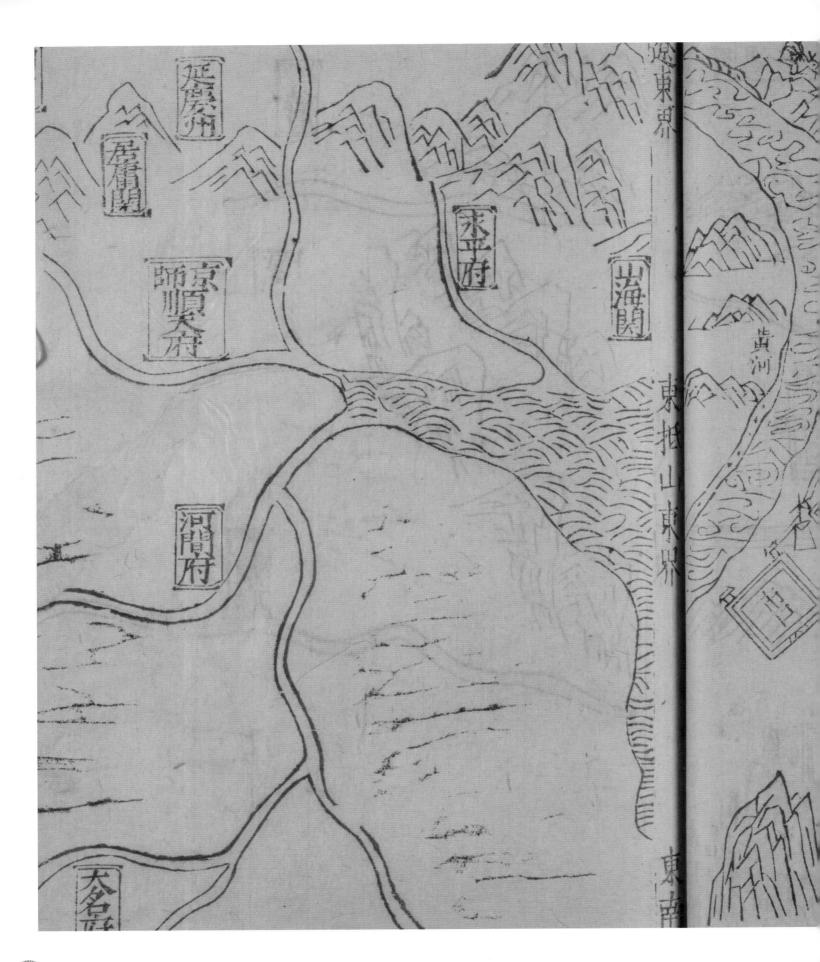

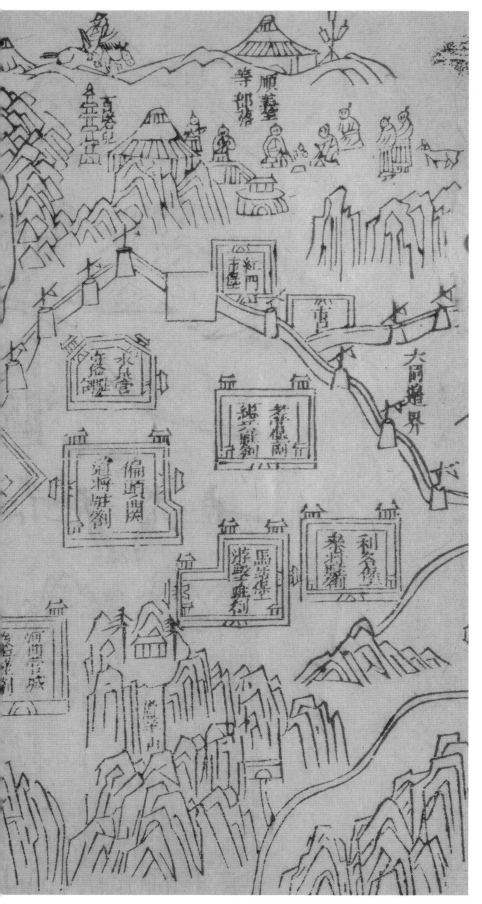

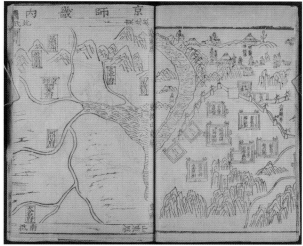

DA MING YITONG ZHI

The Da Ming yitong zhi or 'Comprehensive gazetteer of the Great Ming' was based on more than 40 years' work gathering information, and completed in 1461. The gazetteer starts with a map of the whole of China, but includes only 13 others among its 2,800 leaves – cartography does not seem to have been privileged over text for providing geographical information. The charts in Da Ming yitong zhi are rather less accurate than in the Yu ji tu stone stele (see page 24) made over 300 years earlier; they give a less detailed depiction of rivers and the coastline.

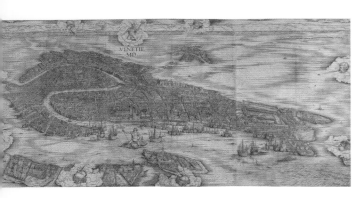

VENICE,
JACOPO DE' BARBARI

This astonishing bird's-eye view of Venice, Italy, was drawn by Jacopo de' Barbari and published in 1500. It would have been even more astonishing to de' Barbari's contemporaries as it was the first aerial view of a city. The bird's-eye view required a leap of faith – the observer could never check the view against their own experience as they could in an oblique elevation, because it was impossible to be above the city. For the first time, it allowed a city to be grasped as a whole, with its own organic shape and structure, rather than as a collection of buildings seen from a particular, slightly elevated standpoint.

The map is 2.8 m (9 ft 2 in) wide by 1.3 m (4 ft 3 in) tall, made from six woodblocks and printed on the largest sheets of paper that had ever been used by European printers. It was based on an exhaustive survey of the city's buildings, canals and paths, with almost every building visible, and took three years to complete.

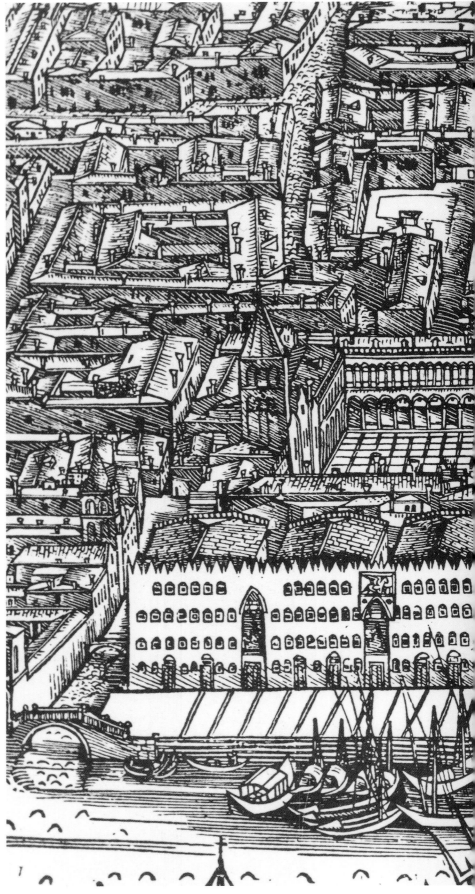

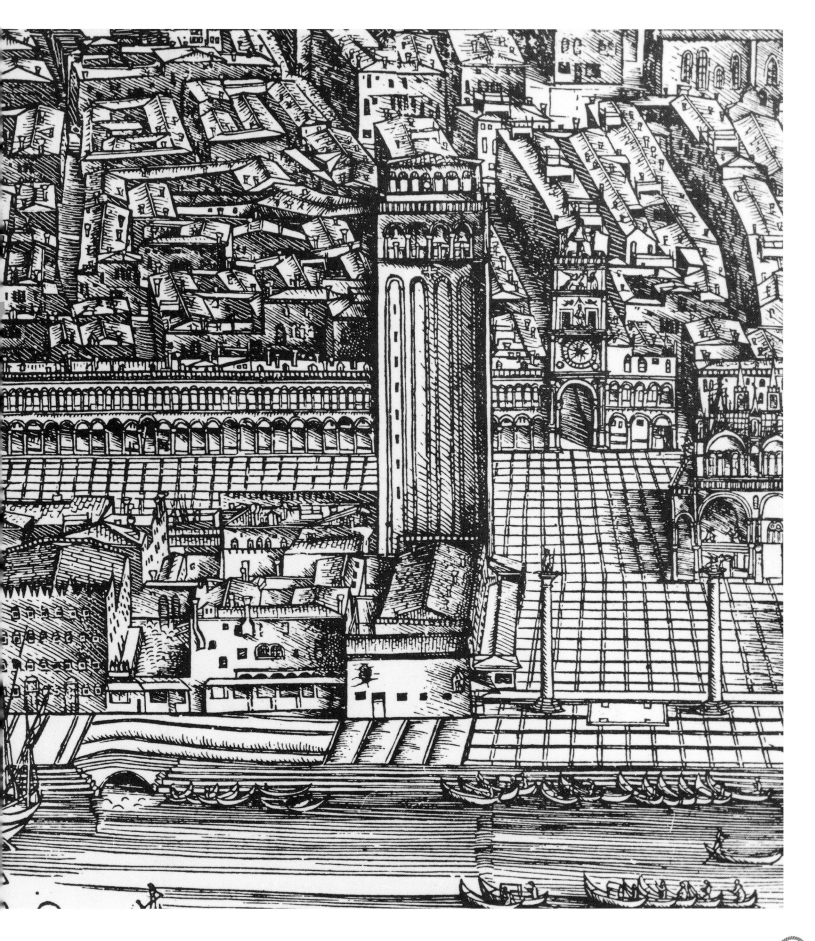

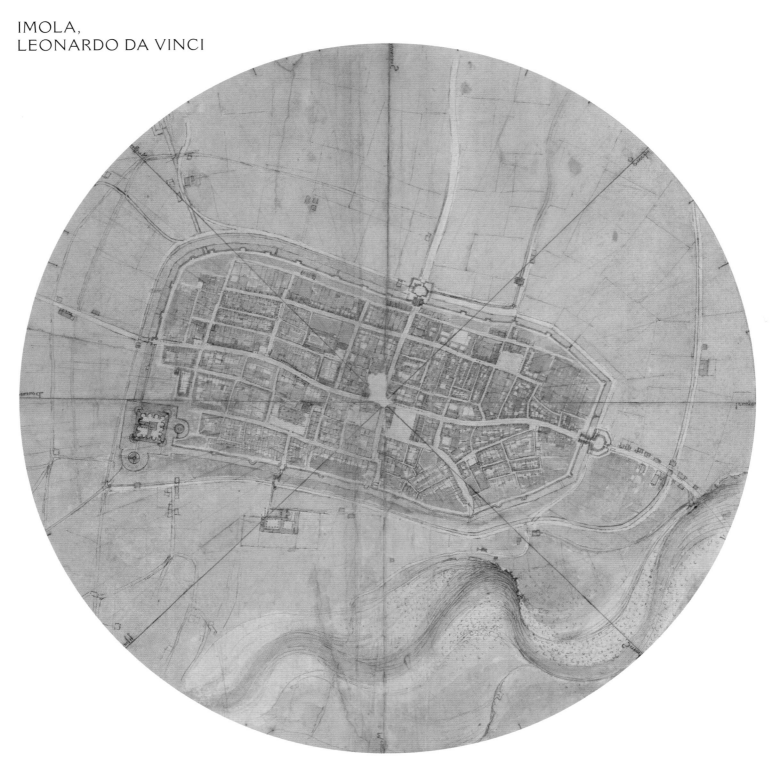

Another revolutionary shift was represented by the plan view. This view of Imola, Italy, was drawn by Leonardo da Vinci in 1502, using ink and watercolour washes. It conforms to the modern idea of a map, with the city walls, streets, rivers, buildings and fields all drawn from directly above. The plan implies not a single point of vision, but infinite points, so that all points on the ground can be observed.

The map is accurate and detailed, with every building and plot of land shown. It was drawn to scale, the distances measured by pacing, using knotted ropes, or with a hodometer. Leonardo's notebooks record designs for the hodometer, an instrument with a wheel of known circumference that is rolled over the ground.

TENOCHTITLÁN, CODEX MENDOZA

Mesoamerican maps combine representations of time (history) and space. The Codex Mendoza, an Aztec map of Tenochtitlán drawn in the 1540s, shows the city as it was near its foundation in 1325. The cactus growing out of a rock in the centre represents the name of the city, the blue page border represents the lakes that mark its geographic space, and the main canals are represented by the blue cross.

Rather than depicting the actual geography, the map shows the social perception of the city, seen by its inhabitants as divided into four quadrants. Outside the lake border, a series of numbered blocks represents its history (not shown). The eagle alighting on the cactus shows the city's mythic origins, when an eagle sent by the deity Huitzilopochtli indicated to the Culhua-Mexica clan where to found the city.

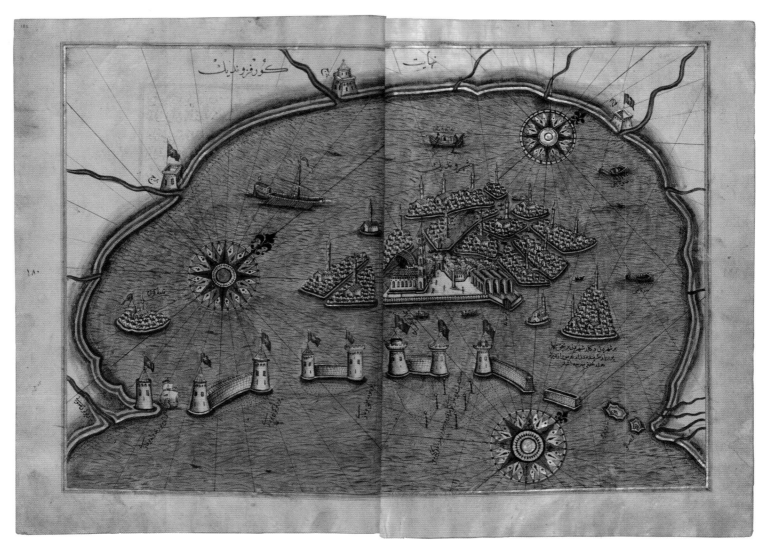

VENICE, PIRI REIS

Piri Reis was a cartographer and admiral in the Ottoman navy who compiled a book of exquisite charts and sailing instructions called the *Kitab-ı Bahriye* (*Book of Navigation*) in 1525. These were portolan charts, intended for use by navigators (see page 89). They did not generally show the interior of the land in any detail, but this view of Venice breaks with tradition to show the city, threaded by canals that make it appear built on the sea, in all its beauty. The jewel-bright colours of the inks are offset with gold.

TENOCHTITLÁN, CORTÉS MAP

This map was created as a woodblock to be printed alongside Hernán Cortés's description of the Aztec capital Tenochtitlán in his second letter to Charles V of Spain in 1524. It is the first European map of the city.

The map is drawn from Cortés's description, including the aviaries (represented by the caged birds beneath the central temple precinct). Although the map shows an Aztec city, it's drawn within the conventions of European map-making: the houses and activity on the lake could be Venetian. The temple precinct is disproportionately large. The city is connected to the shore of the lake by a series of causeways. Other cities are shown on the shores of the lake.

TABRIZ, IRAN, MATRAKÇI NASUH

Matrakçı Nasuh, a multi-talented polymath, swordsman and sharp-shooter, was a Bosnian Muslim recruited into the Ottoman navy. He produced important work in geometry and mathematics, and spoke five languages. One of his books of historical miniatures covered Suleiman I's Iran-Iraq campaign in 1534–5, depicting each of the cities the troops passed through. Tabriz, shown here, is in northwest Iran. The landscape is shown in plan view, but the buildings, bridges and trees are drawn as elevations.

This aerial view of Vienna at the time of the first siege by the Turks in 1529 was created by Hans Sebald Beham. It forms part of a tradition of siege views of cities, in which the drama is as much religious as military. Beham has missed out most of the buildings that are not churches and used the space to show fortifications, so giving the impression of a Christian citadel defending itself against unChristian attackers. There is no hint of ordinary life, though the civic pride that characterizes many city views and plans is clear to see.

TULTEPEC AND JALTOCÁN REGIONS, MEXICO, AYERS MANUSCRIPT

This map is included in a document outlining a legal judgment in a dispute over land between a sheep rancher and Indians from Jaltocán. The land is between Lake Zumpango and Lake Jaltocán, south of the Santa Inés Hacienda, roughly 32 km (20 miles) north of Mexico City. It is drawn in pen and ink and watercolour on amatl paper (made from fig tree fibre). East is at the top; the map is not drawn to scale.

AMMASSALIK COAST OF GREENLAND, KUNIT FRA UMIVIK

The Inuit of Greenland carved maps of the coastline and of series of islands from lumps of wood. This map, carved by Kunit fra Umivik in or before the 1880s, is of the coastline of Ammassalik; it continues all round the piece of wood, up one side and down the other. The map would have been kept in the Inuit sailor's kayak and could be used inside a fur mitten, allowing navigation by touch. The air and water in this region are so cold that to remove the mittens while rowing presents a danger of frostbite. A painted or drawn map would also be in danger of damage from seawater. The tactile wooden maps were resilient and long-lasting.

The map reveals more than just the contours of the coast. Detail on the surface shows the locations of old houses, which made good places for bringing the boat to land, and where a kayak could be carried overland when the sea route was blocked by ice.

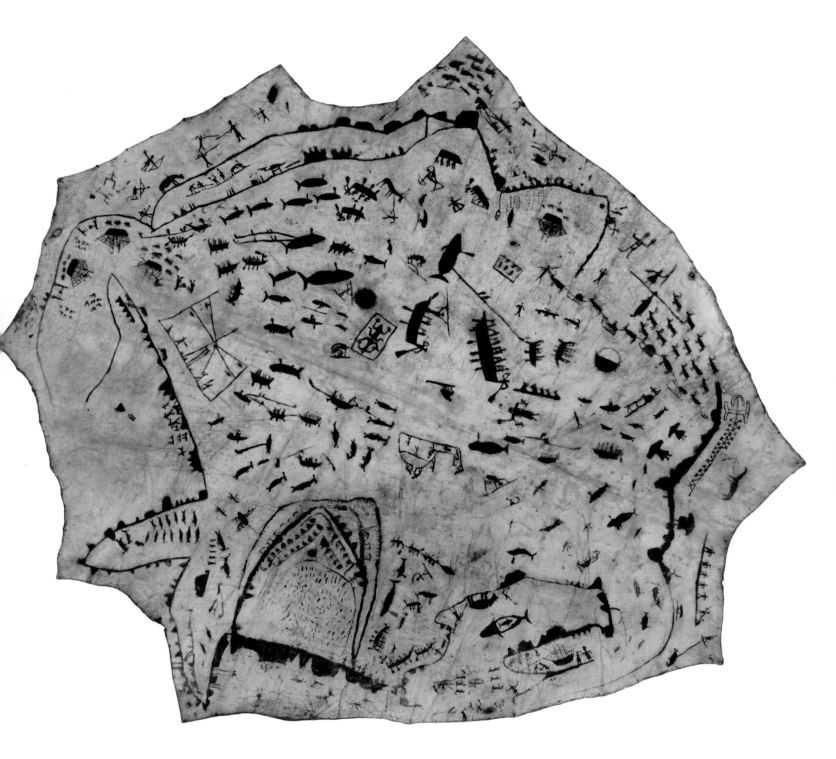

CHUKCHI PENINSULA

This depiction of the coast of the Chukchi peninsula painted on sealskin was bought by the crew of an American whaling vessel around 1870. Experts are divided as to whether it represents a map or an incidental collection of details of Chukchi life. The Chukchi peninsula is in the far east of Russia, just across the sea from Alasaka. Locations including Plover Bay, Chaplino, Michigme and St Lawrence Bay are all shown, as are images of hunting whales, walrus, bears and seals, together with Chukchi settlements and fighting scenes.

SHINPAN
SETTSU OSAKA

The Shinpan settsu Osaka is the oldest surviving printed plan of Osaka (now Tokyo), made in 1655. It is a woodcut, presented as a hanging scroll. East is at the top, following an established tradition of putting the castle at the top of the map. This was a type of map intended for general public use, not for administrative purposes. Tradesmen's homes in the streets of the city are printed in black, but the map gives pictorial representations of places of interest, such as shrines, temples and historic sites, both inside the castle walls and outside the city. The plan was not based on a survey, but is just a diagrammatic representation of the layout of the city.

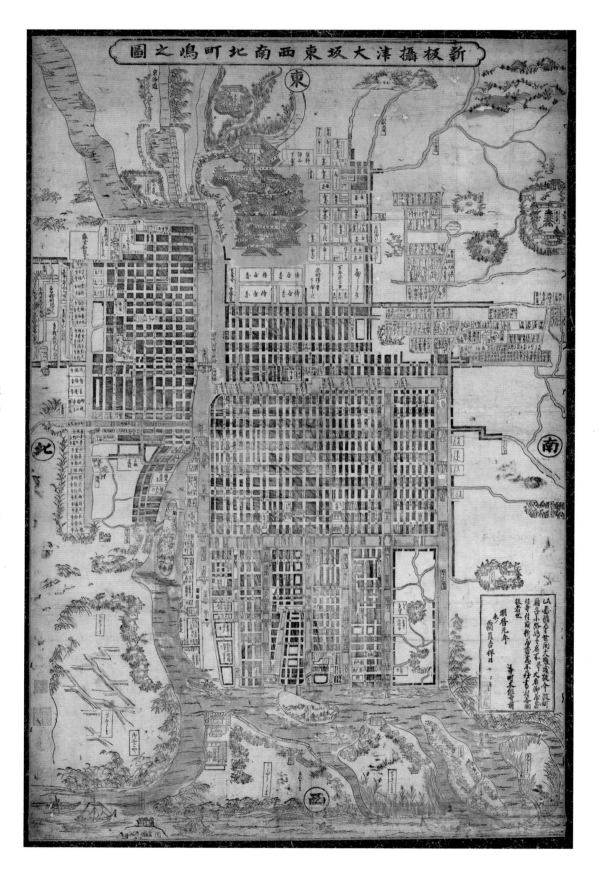

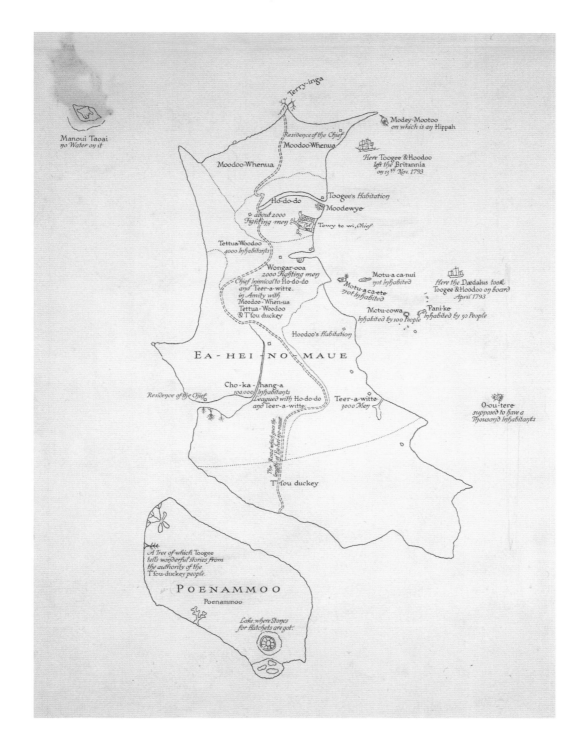

The map contains the following handwritten labels:

Terry-inga

Manoui Taoai
no Water on it

Modey-Mootoo
on which is an Hippah

Residence of the Chief
Moodoo-Whenua

Here Toogee & Hoodoo
left the Britannia
on 13th Nov. 1793

Moodoo-Whenua

Toogee's Habitation

Ho-do-do
Moodewye

about 2000
Fighting men

Towy to wi, Chief

Tettua-Woodoo
4000 Inhabitants

Wongar-ooa
2000 Fighting men
Chief Inimical to Ho-do-do
and Teer-a-witte.
in Amity with
Moodoo-When-ua
Tettua-Woodoo
& T'fou duckey

Motu-a-ca-nui
not Inhabited

Here the Dædalus took
Toogee & Hoodoo on board
April 1793

Motu-a-ca-ete
not Inhabited

Motu-cowa
Inhabited by 100 People

Pani-ke
Inhabited by 50 People

Hoodoo's Habitation

EA-HEI-NO-MAUE

Cho-ka-fhang-a
100,000 Inhabitants
Leagued with Ho-do-do
and Teer-a-witte

Residence of the Chief

Teer-a-witte
3000 Men

O-ou-tere
supposed to have a
Thousand Inhabitants

The Road which goes the
length of Ea-hei-no-maue

T'fou duckey

A Tree of which Toogee
tells wonderful stories from
the authority of the
T'fou-duckey people.

POENAMMOO
Poenammoo

Lake where Stones
for Hatchets are got.

NEW ZEALAND, TUKI TE TERENUI WHARE PIRAU

This is the oldest known Maori map of New Zealand. It was drawn by Tuki Te Terenui Whare Pirau from accumulated knowledge of the area in 1793. West is at the top. The scale is indeterminate – the Maori had no units for measuring long distances. The offshore islands are not shown.

Map-making was an important Maori activity, but it's likely that they produced only ephemeral maps before European explorers and settlers asked them to draw enduring maps. Although this map shows the topography of the main island, the double dotted line shows Te Ara Whânui, the mythical pathway taken by the spirits of the Maori dead to get to a sacred tree (shown at the extreme west). From the sacred tree, the dead spirit could descend to the underworld, Rarohênga.

JIANGXI PROVINCE, CHINA

This 18th-century prefectural map of Jiangxi in southeast China is painted on silk. A total of 7 m (23 ft) long, it was designed to be looked at in sections, partly folded and partly laid out on a table. It uses variable perspective, combining a tilted ground plane with features such as mountains shown in elevation.

The map shows the historic divisions of the individual prefectures, the roads, the rivers and river crossings. The Yangtze river is at the area's northern boundary. Towns are shown as walled settlements; the prominence given to government buildings and Confucian schools indicates the administrative purpose of the map.

NEW LONDON, CHRISTOPHER WREN

In 1666, the Great Fire of London laid waste most of the original walled city, leaving devastated smoking ruins. The prominent architect Christopher Wren leapt into the breach with an ambitious plan to redesign and modernize the city in the style of Paris, with its classically influenced wide avenues and open squares. But Wren failed to take account of the topography of the city, and much of his plan was never feasible. The phoenix in the upper left suggests that London could be reborn from its own ashes – which, indeed, it was, but not following Wren's grandiose plan. The map remains an image of a London that would never be realized. This is a 1744 copy of the original plan, which has been lost.

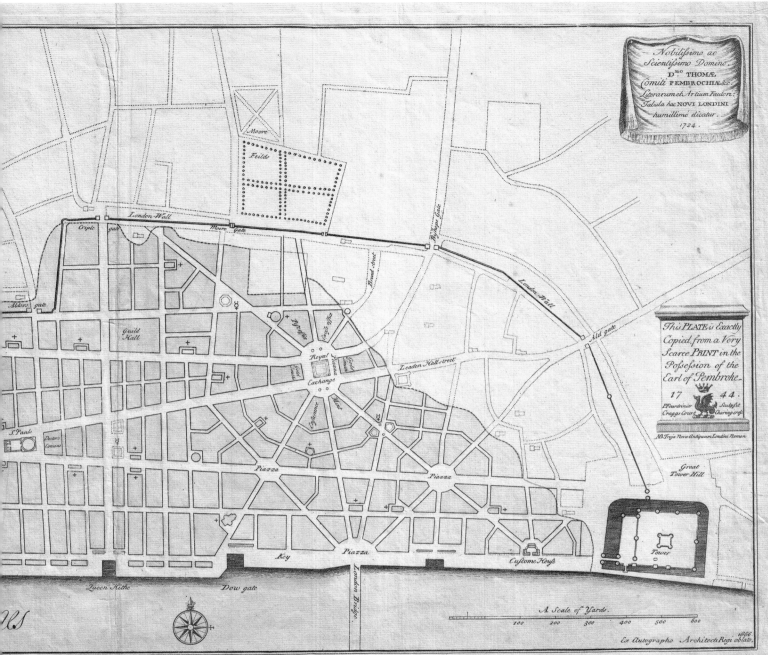

This PLATE is Exactly
Copied, from a Very
Scarce PRINT in the
Poſſeſſion of the
Earl of Pembroke.
17 44.
P.Fourdrinier   Sculpſit
Craggs Court   Charing croſs.
N.B. Troja Nova Antiquum Londini Nomen.

Novæ Urbis
q Ædiſiciorum
c Modulum Novæ
rum Diluvio non
ate Turres ejus

A PLAN of the City of LONDON, after the great FIRE in the Year of OUR LORD 1666. with the MODELL of the New
City, according to the Deſign, and Propoſal of S.r CHRISTOPHER WREN K.t &c. for Rebuilding thereof. Approv'd by y.e King.
NB. The right and right angular Lines &c. ſhew the Model of the New City. — The Short Lines colour'd ſhew the whole Confines of
the Burning. — The Prickt Lines ſhew the Parts of the Old Town which eſcaped the Flames. (+) the Parochial Churches. – (§). Markets. —
Walk about Sion tell the Towers thereof: Mark well her Bulwarks, Set up her Houſes, that ye may tell them that come after. (Pſalm; 48.)

EXPLANATION OF THE PLAN

a Streight and wide Street croſſes the Valley paſſing by the South ſide of LUDGATE, and thence in a direct line through y.e whole City terminates at TOWER-HILL; but
ht Ways, where at one ſtation we ſee (I) ſtraight forward quite through the CITY: (II) Obliquely towards the Right hand, to the beginning of the KEY that runs from
the THAMES: (V) ſtreight on the Left to HATTEN STREET and CLARKENWELL: (VI) ſtreight Backwards towards TEMPLE-BARR: (VII) Obliquely on the Right to the
ty, once ſullied with an offenſive Sewer, now beautified with a uſefull Canal, with Wharfs on each ſide, paſſable by as many Bridges as Streets that croſs it: Leaving LUDGATE,
XCHANGE, and before theſe two Streets ſpreading at Acute Angles can be clear of one another, They form a Triangular Piazza, the Baſes of which is filled by the CATHEDRAL
VER. We return again to LUDGATE, and leaving S.t PAULS on the Right hand, paſs along the other great Branch to the ROYAL EXCHANGE; Seated in the Place where it was,
the South Front; and another from HOLBORN over the Canal to NEWGATE, and thence ſtreight to the North Front. &c. Inſtead of LUDGATE-PRISON was Deſigned a

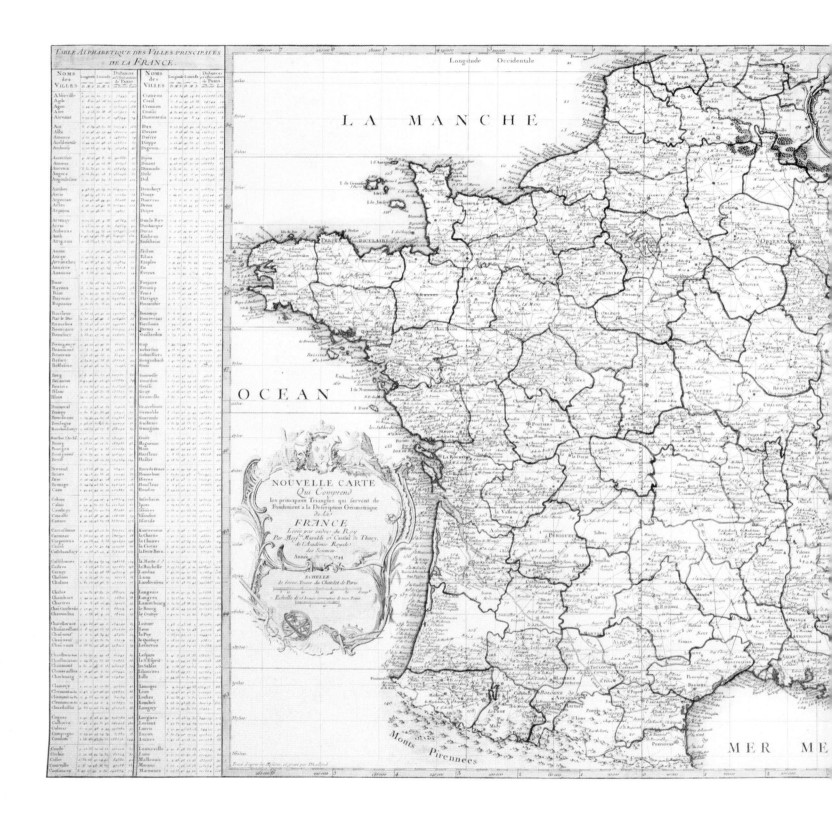

The first official map of the whole of France was started by César-François Cassini and finished by his son, Jean-Dominique, during the 18th century. Cassini (who was Director of the Paris Observatory) timed eclipses of Jupiter's moons in Paris and Brest to work out the longitude of the cities. He sent surveyors all over the country, using geodetic triangulation for the first time; some were attacked, and one even murdered by wary locals. It set the standard for all subsequent large-scale mapping projects.

Cassini found France to be 20 per cent smaller than all previous estimates, an embarrassing discovery for a project steeped in national pride and supported personally by the king. The French Revolution took place before the map was complete, and the revolutionaries immediately claimed the map as national property and used it to draw new boundaries within France.

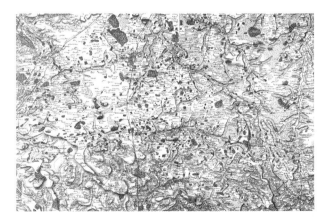

The maps adopted standardized symbols for features. They did not aim to show dwellings and other buildings, as previous maps generally did, but to show the unchanging features of the landscape (mountains, rivers and so on, but not swamps and woods) and the route of roads. The Cassinis' team accomplished this with astonishing accuracy – comparison with modern satellite images reveals few errors. Published over the period 1744–93, the 182 plates that make up the Cassini map represented the most detailed and accurate mapping project ever undertaken.

VESUVIUS, CAMPI PHLEGRAEI, WILLIAM HAMILTON

William Hamilton was a diplomat stationed in Naples, Italy, where he also studied volcanology. His cartographic picture of the Campi Phlegraei, the volcanic area around Naples, is dominated by the destructive eruption of Mount Vesuvius in 1760–1. The striking image of half-map, half-destruction that will remould the landscape underlines the contingent nature of all maps.

THE PACIFIC ISLANDS, TUPAIA

This map of the islands of the Pacific was drawn in 1769–70 by Captain James Cook, either under the direction of the Tahitian navigator Tupaia or working from an original drawn by Tupaia. Tupaia was renowned for his knowledge of the islands of the Pacific, and his map was lauded at the time of its creation, apparently showing that he knew islands over an area larger than the United States. But there are many errors, especially in the placing of the islands furthest from Tahiti. Some errors – but not all – can be accounted for by Cook's misunderstanding of how Tahitians indicate direction.

Tupaia had not drawn a map before seeing the European charts. Half of the islands he included were not known to Western sailors at the time. The size of the islands relates to their importance in legend and history, not to their physical geography. Tahitian navigators knew when they were close to or far from islands by the presence of different types of fish and birds. Tupaia steered the *Endeavour* through part of the Pacific, having agreed to accompany Cook to Britain, but died of illness in Jakarta.

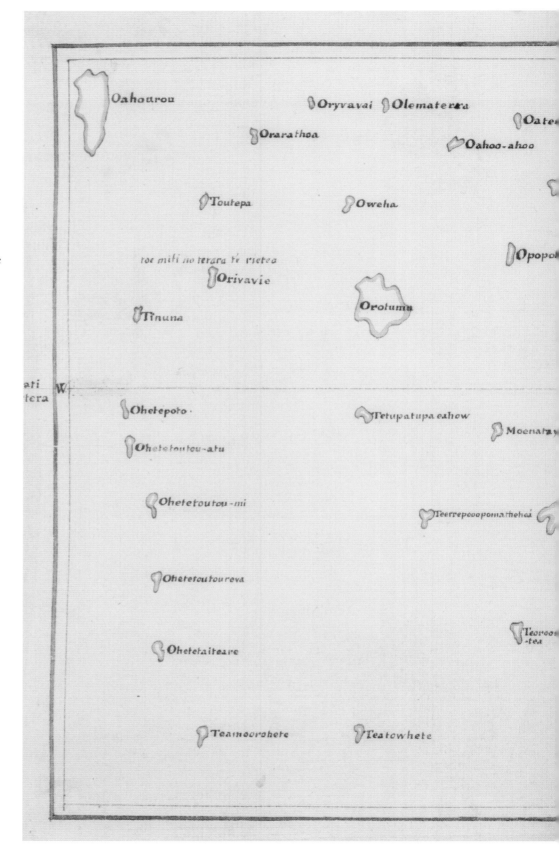

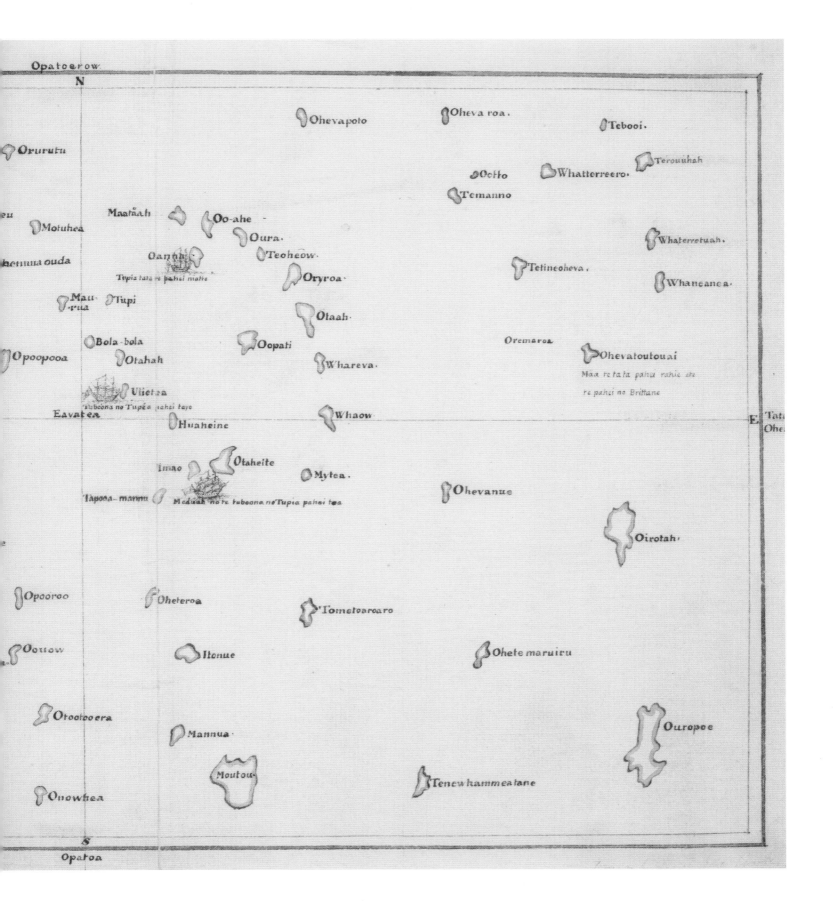

Opatoerow.

N

Ohevapoto

Oheva roa.

Tebooi.

Orurutu

Ootto

Whatterreero.

Terouuhah

Temanno

Maataah

Oo-ahe

eu

Motuhea

Oura.

Whaterretuah.

Teoheow.

henuua ouda

Oanu

Oryroa.

Tetineoheva.

Whaneanea.

Tupia tata re pahei matte

Mau
rua

Tupi

Otaah.

Bola-bola

Oopati

Oremaroa

Ohevatoutouai

Opoopooa

Otahah

Whareva.

Maa re tata pahei rahie ete

Uliet2a

re pahei no Brittane

Tuboona no Tupea pahei tayo

Eavatea

Whaow.

E. Tata
Ohe

Huaheine

Imao

Otaheite

Tapooa-mannu

Mytea.

Ohevanue

Medtah no te tuboona no Tupia pahei tea

Oirotah.

Opooroo

Oheteroa

Tometoaroaro

Oouow

Itonue

Ohete maruiru

Otootooera

Ouropoe

Mannua

Onowhea

Moutou

Tenewhammeatane

S

Opatoa.

The next country after France to take on a monumental national mapping project was Great Britain. The Ordnance Survey began with a detailed map of Scotland, proposed in 1746 to help the army and government subjugate the clans. This first project used a scale of 1 inch:1000 yards, or 1:36,000. The mapping of England and Wales began properly in 1790 with the south coast. The first map, at one inch to a mile, was published in 1801 and showed Kent. The whole project was measured from a baseline that ran through Hounslow (and is now partly under Heathrow Airport). The baseline was accurate to 7.5 cm in 8 km (about 3 inches in 5 miles). The longest-serving director of the project, Thomas Colby, joined in with the legwork, helping to build camps, carry out surveys, and organize post-survey parties with giant plum puddings.

BROOMFIELDS, 1893

The Ordnance Survey maps continue to be developed and corrected, right up to the present day. This portion of an OS map showing Broomfields, near Bradford, in 1893 shows the densely packed housing that sprang up in cities to accommodate the working classes during the Industrial Revolution.

ST COLUMB MAJOR, CORNWALL, 1810

This sketch, by one of the original surveyors for the Ordnance Survey, shows St Columb in Cornwall oriented with southeast to the top. Detailed sketches formed the basis of the maps. This one marks tin and copper mines (the key shows how to distinguish between them) and marks the birthplace of the portrait painter John Opie, 'Harmony Cot'. This type of personal anecdotal material was not included in the final maps.

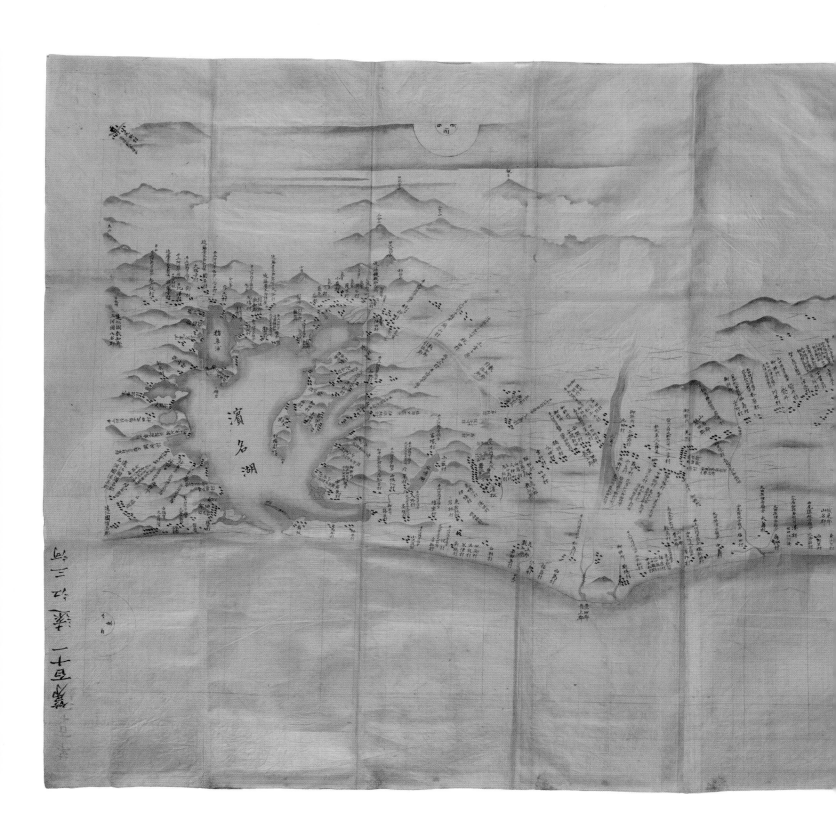

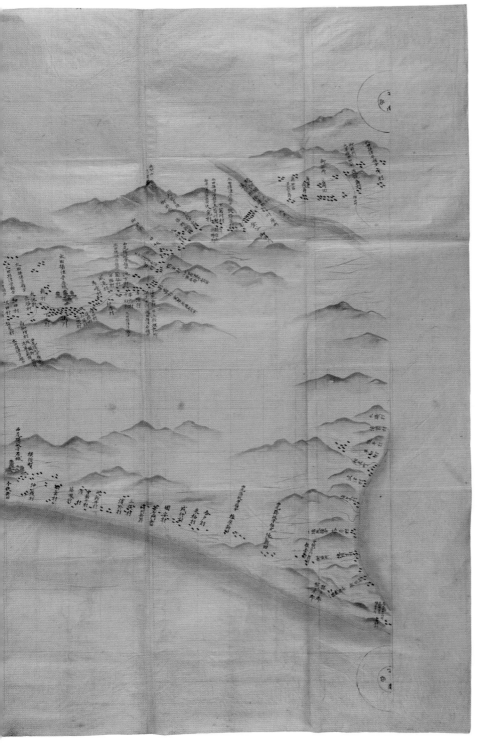

Inō Tadataka (1745–1818) is considered the father of modern map-making in Japan. In 1800, using his own money, he undertook a thorough survey of the land for the first time, spending 3,736 days making measurements. Overall, he spent 17 years mapping Japan, compiling a book that contained large-scale maps of the whole country spread over three pages, and 214 pages of more detailed maps of the coastline. He died before the project was finished, but his surveying team completed it. The maps, accurate to within a thousandth of a degree, were in use until the early 20th century.

CHAPTER 2

OVER LAND & SEA

***An important use of maps has always been
to plan or record a journey.***

A JOURNEY IS EXPERIENCED as a single line followed, from which surrounding topographic features are more or less visible. Itinerary maps convert this experience of a journey into a means of representing it, showing the route straightened out into a single line from one point to another (like the strip maps on page 78). This privileges the path of the traveller over the lie of the land, and is more a geographical to-do list than a map. Other route maps use the form more familiar to us, of a planimetric, stylized view of the landscape with the route marked as a straight or winding path as it would appear seen from above. Interestingly, the view we see on a sat nav is a return to the sequence-view of early itinerary and strip maps. Distance is important, but the time spent is often of more interest than how far has been travelled. Many route maps and itineraries have given travelling time rather than distance between stages.

ROUTE TO ROSTAU, THE BOOK OF THE TWO WAYS

This map is painted inside the wooden outer coffin of Gua, a physician, from Deir el-Bersha, Egypt. It was made during the 12th Dynasty (2040-1750 BC). The map is part of the Book of the Two Ways, a precursor to the Book of the Dead, and shows the two alternative routes to Rostau, the abode of Osiris, the destination of the dead person's spirit. The two routes, one by water (the blue line on the right) and one by land (the black line to the left of it), are separated by an orange lake of fire.

THERA FRESCO, SANTORINI, c.1500 BC

Although its main purpose was decorative and narrative, these fragments of a fresco in the House of the Admiral at Akrotiri on the Greek island of Santorini preserve map views from c.1500 BC. One shows an oblique view of a sea journey, with a fleet of ships leaving a town and travelling to its home port. Another shows a river in plan view, with flora and fauna along the banks. The rivers are shown in blue with a gold outline.

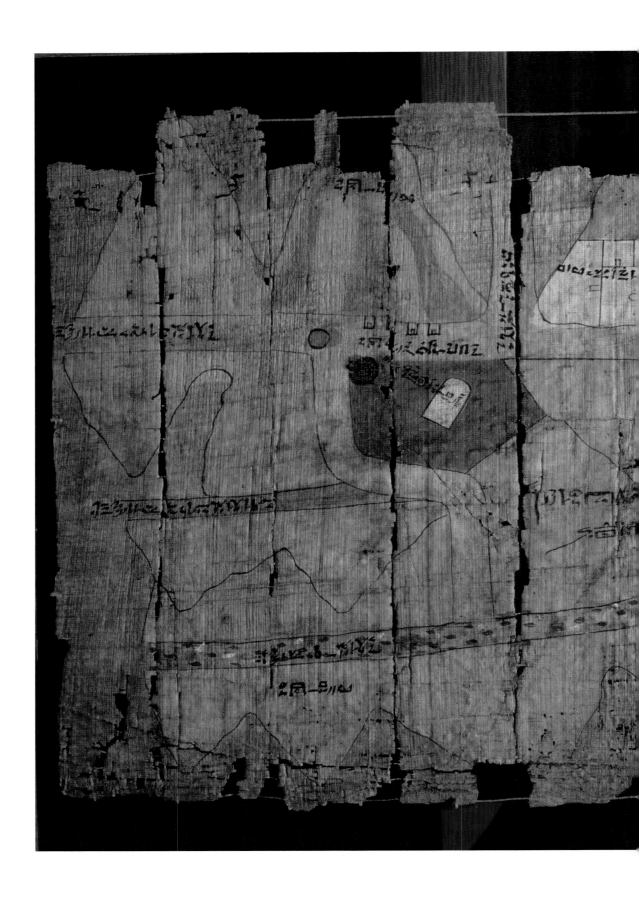

TURIN PAPYRUS

This fragment of a map from c.1165 BC shows a route to gold-bearing mountains in Nubia, south of Egypt. The map, drawn on papyrus, uses red colouring to show 'the mountains where gold is worked'. Annotations suggest that it might have been used to indicate the route for moving stone to be used for statues, or a part-carved statue, to the Valley of the Kings. The exact location shown is not known with certainty, and no scale is indicated on the map.

The section shown depicts roads running between the Nile and the Black Sea. There are mountains (in pink) either side of the roads. The lower road, with its spotty appearance, possibly represents a wadi (dried watercourse); wadis formed natural roads across the desert during dry periods. The text labelling in hieratic indicates where the roads go and which of the reddish-coloured mountains can be mined for gold and silver. The white shape like a tombstone represents a stone stele cut into the mountain. The larger white shape is labelled 'resting place of Amun of the pure mountain'. The small squares at the foot of a mountain to the left of that are houses in the gold-working settlement.

TABULA PEUTINGERIANA

The Peutinger map is an itinerary map, showing the roads around the lands Romans travelled, with staging posts, large rivers and forests. There are standardized symbols representing spas, grain stores and towns. A total of 104,000 km (65,000 miles) of roads are shown, with distances between staging posts marked. The north–south scale is considerably smaller than the east–west scale, meaning that it is impossible to see the relative distances between places by looking at the map. Total distances are calculated by adding up the distances between staging posts. In the Roman areas, distances are shown in Roman miles, but elsewhere in leagues (in Gaul), parasangs (in Persia) and Indian miles (in India). A league is about 4.8 km (3 miles) and a parasang about 5.6 km (3.5 miles). Originally a single roll of parchment 6.75 m (22 ft) long, the map has been divided into sections for ease of preservation.

The surviving map is a 12th- or 13th-century copy of an original probably made in the 4th century. The original was itself probably copied from a 1st-century map, as Pompeii and Herculaneum are shown, both of which were destroyed in AD 79 by the eruption of Mount Vesuvius.

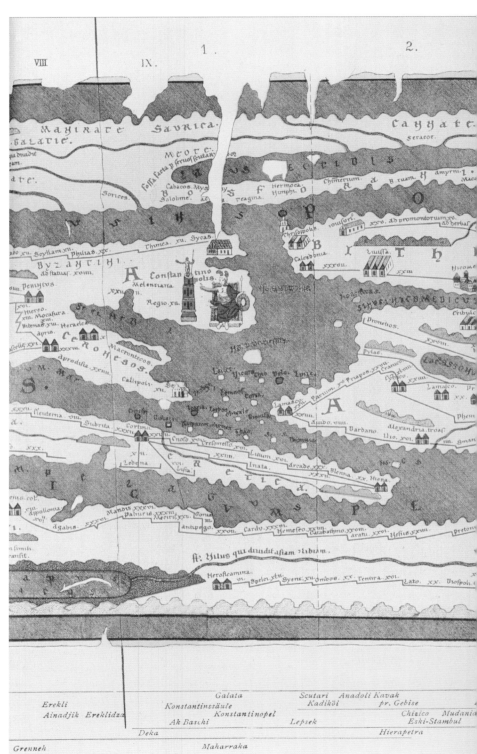

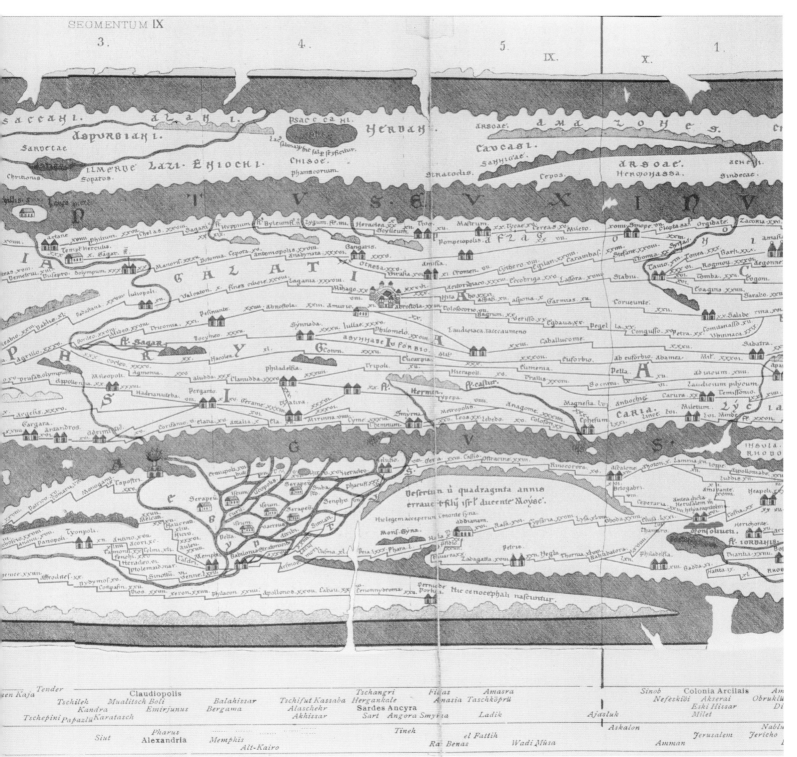

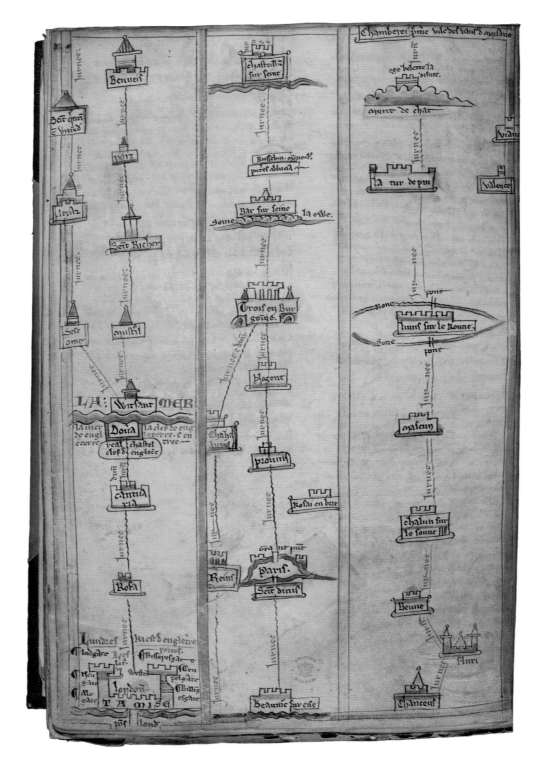

PILGRIMAGE TO THE HOLY LAND, MATTHEW PARIS

Matthew Paris, a Benedictine monk based at St Albans in England, drew an itinerary map of the route from London to the Apulian ports in Italy from where pilgrims embarked by ship for the Holy Land. This first portion shows the route from London to Chambery in France, including crossing the sea (in the first column, labelled 'La Mer').

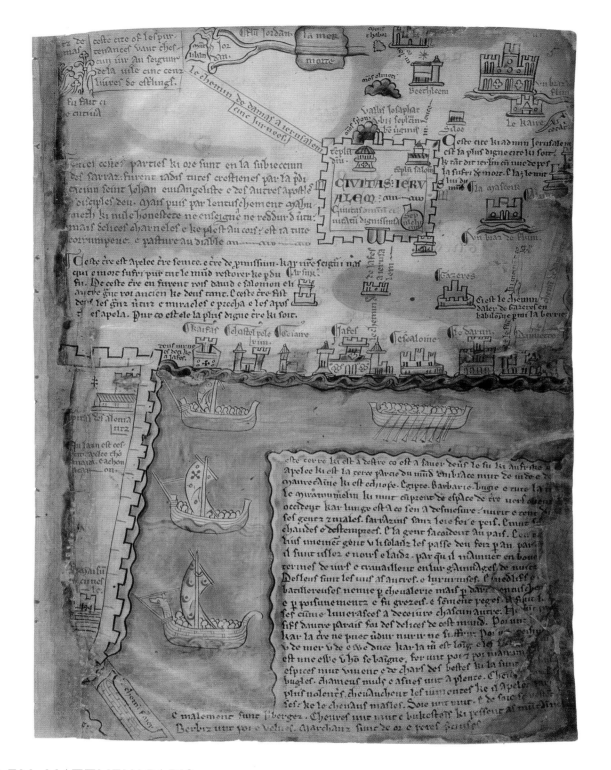

JERUSALEM, MATTHEW PARIS

The final destination of the pilgrimage, Jerusalem, is shown with a planimetric view of roads, rivers and city walls, and buildings in elevation – a common combination for the date. Although his maps give stopping points all the way between London and Rome, with distances marked in days'

travel, it is unlikely that they were ever intended as real travellers' guides. It is more likely that Paris's book of maps was used for a spiritual – or armchair – pilgrimage, guiding the non-traveller's contemplations from the comfort of home or (more likely) monastery.

VOYAGE TO THE HOLY LAND, REUWICH AND BREYDENBACH

Peregrinatio in Terram Sanctam, published in 1497, was the first ever illustrated, printed travel book. Written by Bernhard von Breydenbach and illustrated by Erhard Reuwich, it recorded their pilgrimage to the Holy Land in 1483–4. Their book was a bestseller, and was translated from Latin into several European languages. The pair travelled overland to Venice, then sailed to Corfu, Modon and Rhodes, and on to the Holy Land. The book included five large, fold-out woodcuts, one a 1.5 m (5 ft) view of Venice, and views and maps of other cities. This detail shows the destination, with part of the city of Jerusalem on the right.

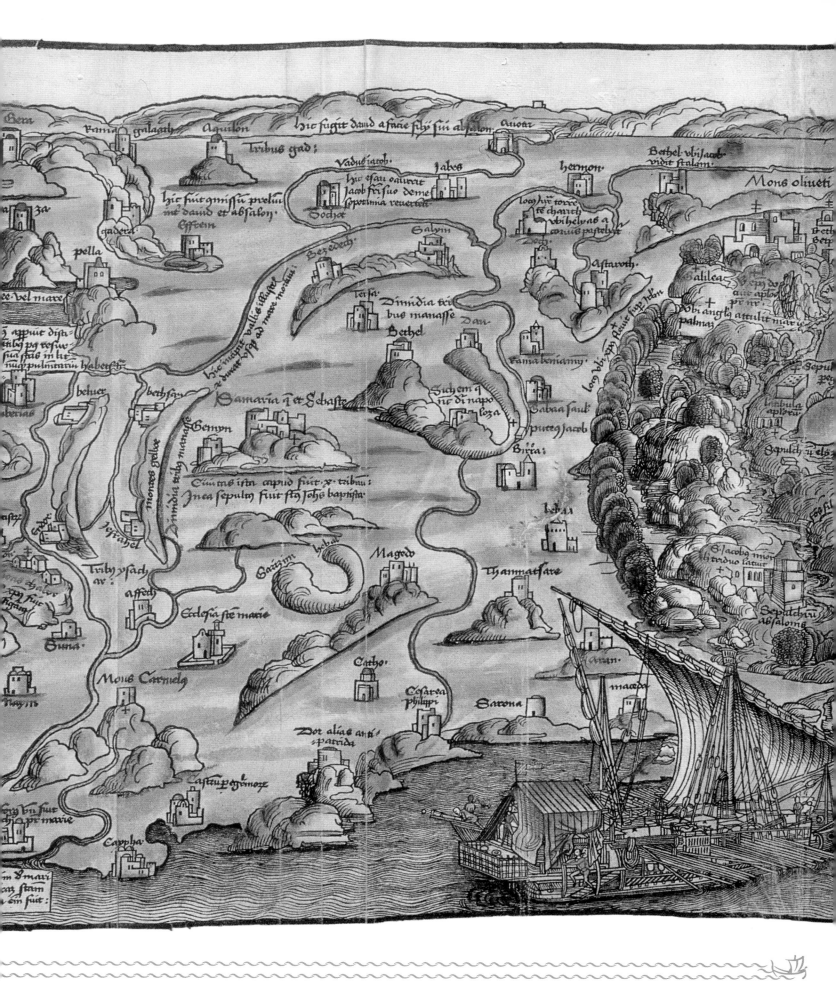

ST LAWRENCE RIVER, CANADA

This map, drawn around 1536 or 1542, depicts one of three journeys made by French navigator Jacques Cartier to explore the St Lawrence river in Canada. Cartier was seeking a new route to Asia and hoping to find gold, spices and other riches. His explorations prepared the way for France to claim Canada later, but were not successful in other ways. He annoyed the Iroquois, who had originally been keen to help him; the putative gold and diamonds he collected turned out to be worthless; and he abandoned the colonists who were following him when he realized the severity of the Canadian winter. However, he did give Canada its name, apparently misunderstanding the Iroquois word 'kanata', meaning village, and applying it to the area around Quebec. It was later adopted for the whole nation.

The main image shows Cartier, in the long, red coat, greeting the local Iroquois. The chart includes the first known use of the word Canada on a map.

BRIXEN, ITALY, GEORG BRAUN AND FRANZ HOGENBERG

The six-volume atlas *Civitates Orbis Terrarum*, published 1572–1619, was not a record of travels but a book of city plans and views that might inspire them. It was, essentially, travel maps for lazy people – armchair travellers who might never embark on a journey at all. Braun and Hogenberg presented 546 cities all around the world, their work intended to be a companion volume to Ortelius's *Theatrum Orbis Terrarum* of 1570 (see page 98). The figures present in most views serve a dual purpose – not only do they show local dress and lifestyle but, according to Braun's introduction, their presence deterred the Muslim Turks from scrutinizing the plans while searching for military secrets, as they were not allowed to look at representations of the human form. This page, showing Brixen in the South Tyrol from a raised position and Lauingen in Bavaria more as elevations, appeared in a late volume, published in 1617.

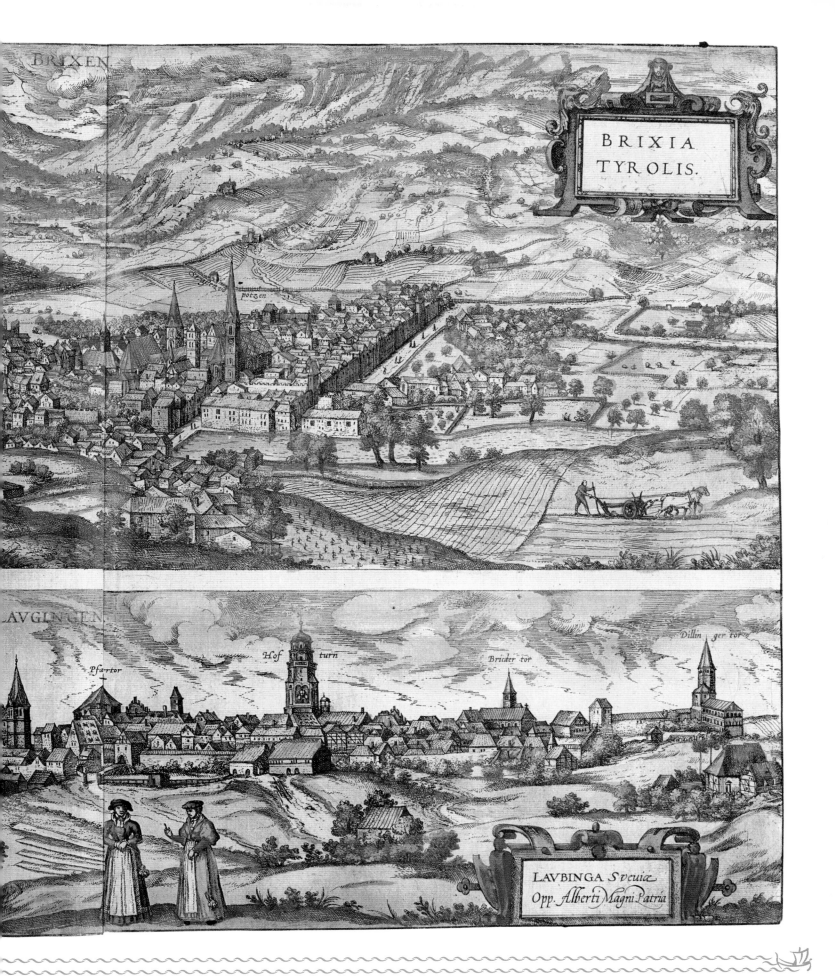

BRIXEN

BRIXIA
TYROLIS.

potzen

LAVGINGEN

Pfarrtor

Hof turn

Bricter tor

Dillin ger tor

LAVBINGA *Sveuiæ*
Opp. Alberti Magni Patria

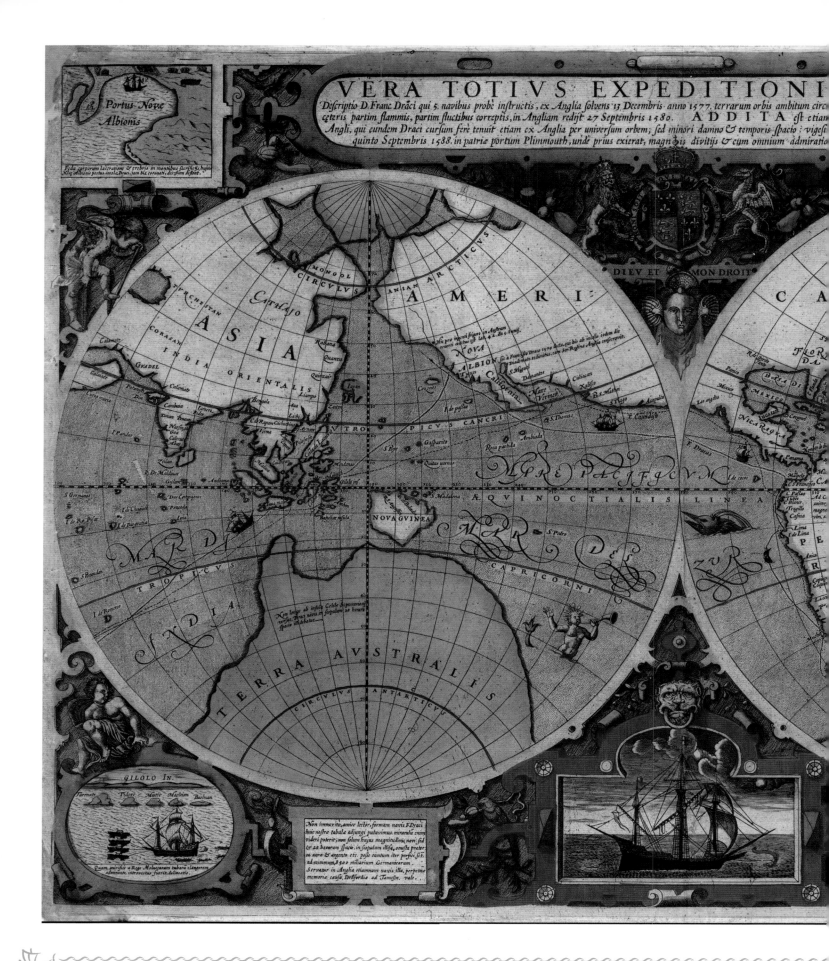

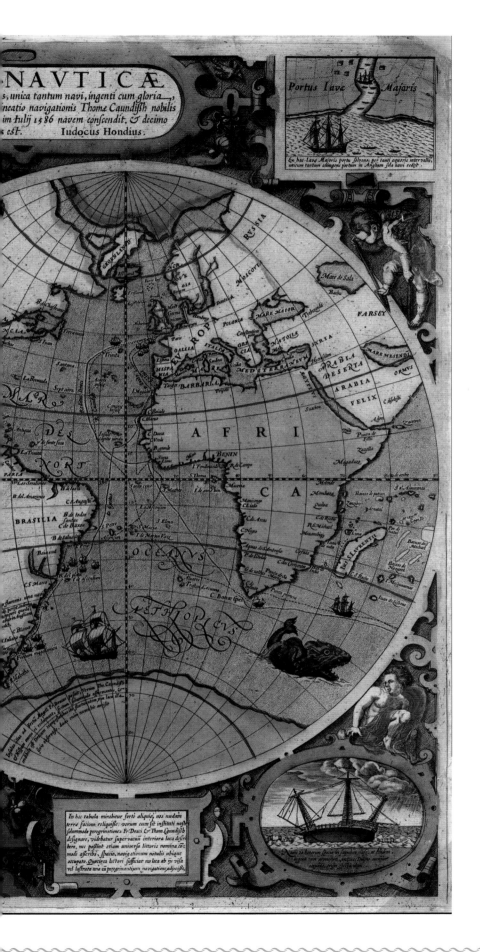

DRAKE'S CIRCUMNAVIGATION OF THE GLOBE, JODOCUS HONDIUS

The Vera Totius Expeditionis Nauticae was made by the Dutch cartographer Jodocus Hondius around 1595. It records the circumnavigation of the globe by Francis Drake in 1577–9 and by Thomas Cavendish in 1586–8. Showing the world as two hemispheres, Atlantic and Pacific views, Hondius's map focuses on the coastlines and shows the interiors of the continents blank, following the pattern of the portolan charts (see page 89). Australia is not shown, having not been discovered by Europeans; the area labelled 'Terra Australis' corresponding to Antarctica is conjectural, based on the theory that there was a large, undiscovered landmass in the southern hemisphere. The paths taken by Drake and Cavendish are marked. The vignettes around the map include Drake's ship, the *Golden Hind* (bottom centre) and Drake's landing at New Albion, present-day California (top left).

STRIP MAP JOURNEYS IN BRITAIN

John Ogilby created the first road atlas of Great Britain in 1675, comprising a set of 100 strip maps detailing routes around the country. The maps were drawn to a scale of one inch to one mile, and Ogilby adopted the standard mile of 1,760 yards instead of the local miles commonly in use. The journeys are marked with distances in miles, subdivided into furlongs. It has been suggested that his atlas was intended to facilitate a Catholic takeover of Britain.

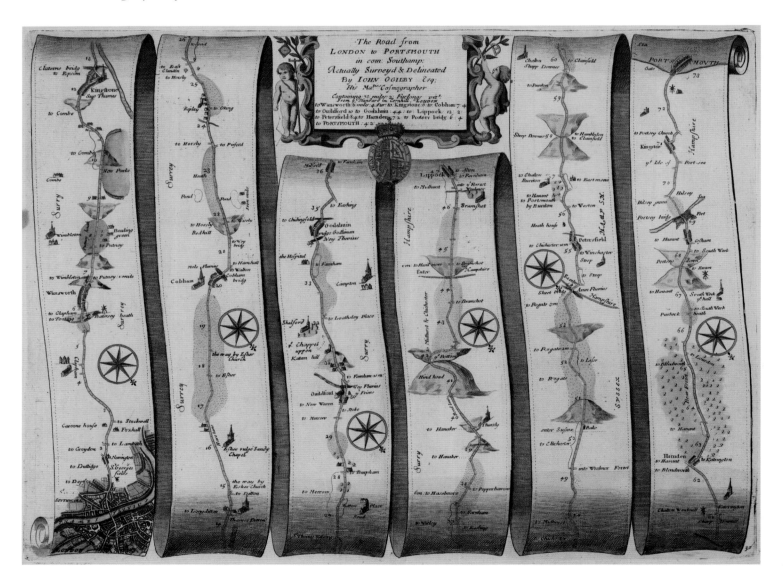

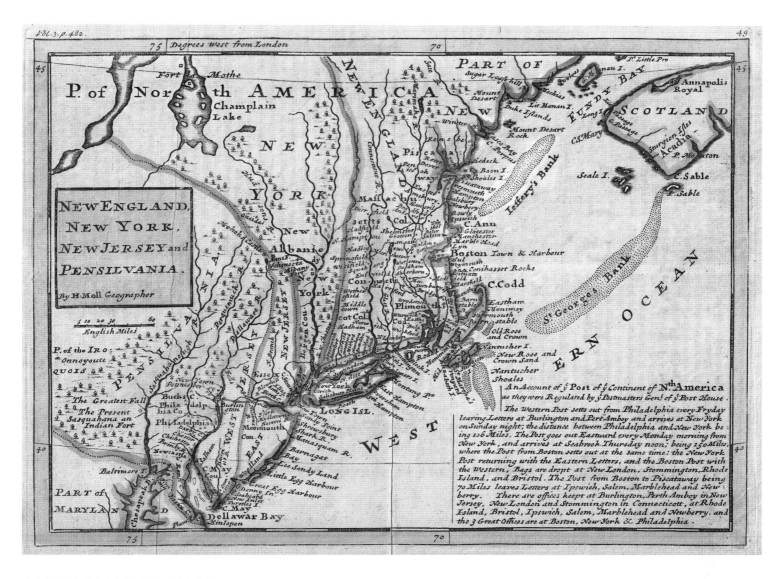

AMERICAN POST MAP

Drawn by Herman Moll in 1729, this map of New England and the adjacent colonies is known as the 'Post Map' because it focuses on the postal system operating around New England, New York, New Jersey and Pennsylvania. The first official postal service began in New England around 1639, when a tavern in Boston was used to receive mail to or from Europe. The first official postal service route, between New York and Boston, began in 1673 and is described in the text panel in the lower right. The route is now US Route 1.

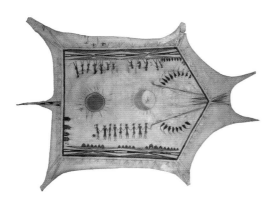

ROUTE OF QUAPAW WARRIORS TO CONFRONT ENEMIES

Possibly the oldest surviving Native American map, this 18th-century depiction on bison hide shows the path taken by Quapaw warriors to confront their enemies. The route goes through three villages and a French settlement, probably Arkansas Post, shown around two sides of the hide. The wiggly part after the last settlement (on the left) might indicate the sinuosity of the actual route, or could be symbolic. At the top of the map, the Quapaw are shown fighting with and defeating the Chickasaws in an area near another settlement. This image represents one of a series of battles between the two tribes in the mid-1740s.

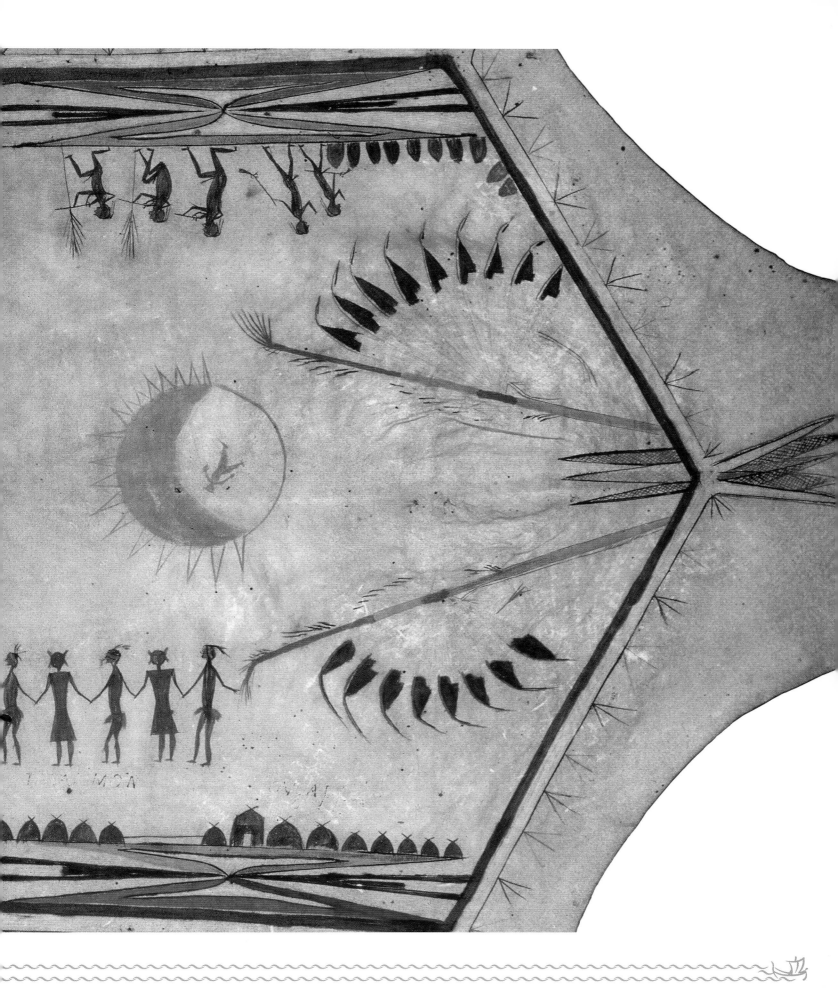

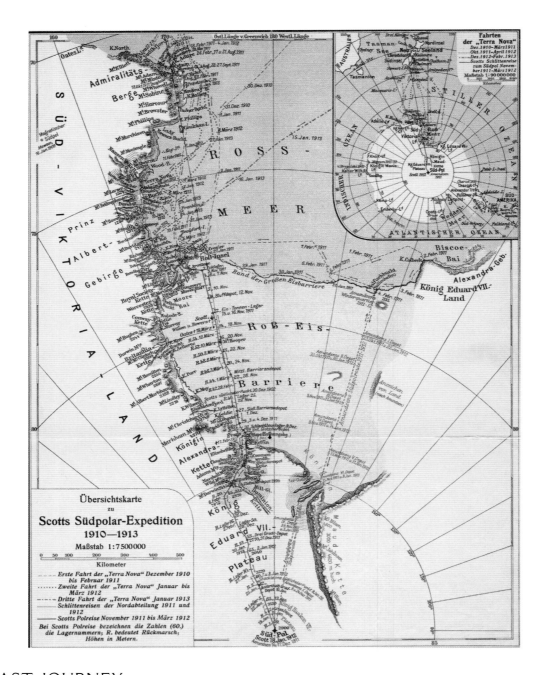

Übersichtskarte
zu
Scotts Südpolar-Expedition
1910—1913

Maßstab 1:7500000

0   50 100   200   300   400   500
Kilometer

---------- Erste Fahrt der „Terra Nova" Dezember 1910
         bis Februar 1911
.... Zweite Fahrt der „Terra Nova" Januar bis
         März 1912
— · — · — Dritte Fahrt der „Terra Nova" Januar 1913
— — — — Schlittenreisen der Nordabteilung 1911 und
         1912
———— Scotts Polreise November 1911 bis März 1912
Bei Scotts Polreise bezeichnen die Zahlen (60.)
die Lagernummern; R. bedeutet Rückmarsch;
Höhen in Metern.

SCOTT'S LAST JOURNEY

At the start of the 20th century, Antarctica remained one of the last places on Earth unmapped. This chart of Scott's final expedition to the South Pole, in 1910–13, shows the route his team took to the Pole, arriving there 34 days after their rival Roald Amundsen. Scott and his team died on the return journey. The route map shows how little was known of Antarctica, with only mountains visible from the route being marked. The different summer and winter coastline, as ice melts or builds up, makes any map of Antarctica season-dependent. The first broadly accurate map was produced in 1983.

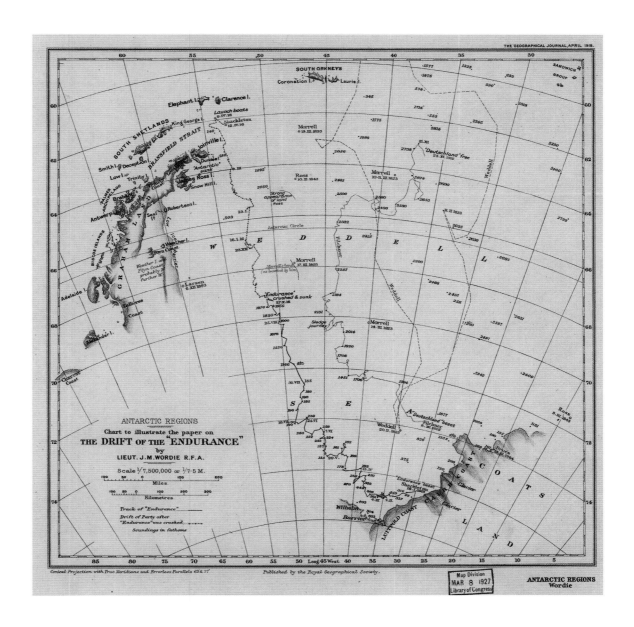

DRIFT OF THE *ENDURANCE*

Despite the disastrous end of Scott's voyage to Antarctica, Shackleton set sail for the continent in *Endurance* in 1914. The journey south through the Weddell Sea was arduous, the passage obstructed by formidable pack ice. Shackleton made a regrettable decision not to land early. *Endurance* was forced off course and became locked in by pack ice in January 1915. The ship drifted with the ice throughout the Antarctic winter before being finally crushed in October. The party then set off overland by sledge, taking their lifeboats.

The map shows the path of the drifting *Endurance* from Coats Land to the place where it was crushed by ice, southeast of Graham Land, and the route taken by the party, up towards the Bransfield Strait and by sea to Elephant Island.

LUKASA

Lukasa, or memory boards, are historical maps depicting the journeys made by kings of the Democratic Republic of Congo. The maps are still used during initiation rites of the Luba, when the board is recited or sung by a *mbudye*, one of the elders of the tribe. The arrangement of beads and shells on the board charts the journeys of a historical king through a landscape. Residences that later become spirit capitals are marked by large beads or cowrie shells; circles of beads mark chieftaincies; lines of beads mark migration routes or paths. The interpretation of the board can vary (for example, the names of spirit centres changing) depending on which king is being celebrated. This example is from the 19th century.

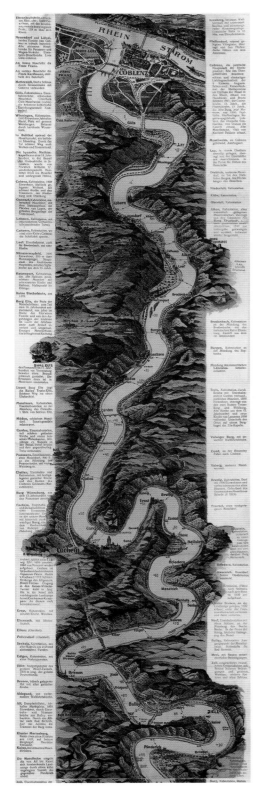

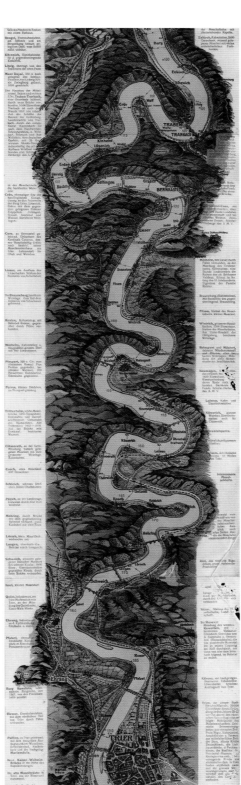

MOSEL, GERMANY

Rivers have always been vital arteries, and maps of rivers have been common for centuries. In the past they were predominantly useful as route maps for delivering goods or travelling, for trade and military expeditions and defence. This example of the path of the River Mosel through Germany was drawn in the 1930s and is intended for leisure and tourism, with historic cities marked, as well as points at which the river can be crossed.

CHAPTER 3

EXPLORATION & EXPANSION

Exploration is a particular type of journey.

SOMETIMES IT HAS A DEFINABLE GOAL, such as Columbus's aim to find a western passage to Asia. At other times it is just to see what's out there. In a sense, any trip to map an area, whether familiar or unknown, is a journey of exploration and discovery – but there is a very real difference between venturing into an alien landscape with no expectations of what you might find and exploring the nooks and crannies of a coastline you or your tribe have lived with for decades.

Maps for explorers and colonists served two main purposes: they were aids to navigation in finding their way to new lands, and they were a record of what was found and, often, claimed. The latter use gave them a political dimension. A map not only shows what is there, but who it belongs to, and the act of mapping can even become an act of claiming ownership.

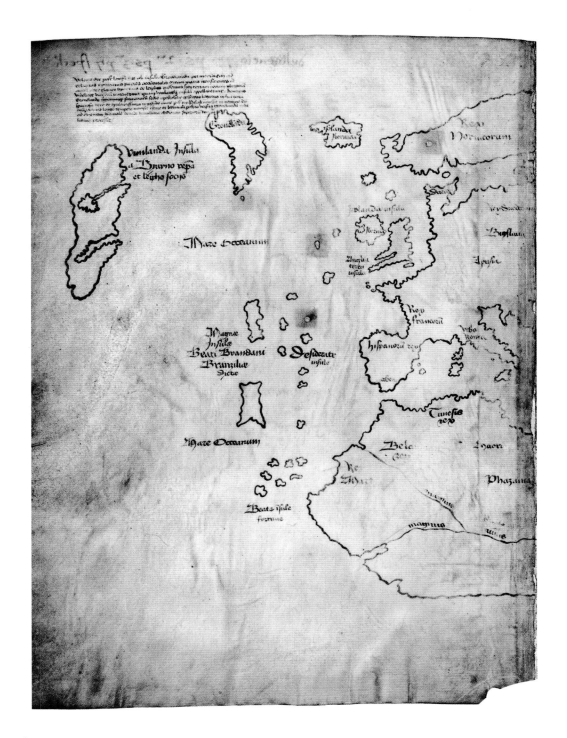

VINLAND MAP

The Vinland map was discovered in 1957 and hailed as evidence that Europeans had sailed to North America before Columbus. The copy was originally dated to the 15th century and includes annotations which claim Europeans first visited in the 11th century. Detailed scientific analysis and academic study have proven fairly conclusively that the map is a fake: a modern chemical is present in one of the inks, and the chart shows more similarity with an engraving made in 1782 of a map produced in 1436 than with the original. The map is drawn on vellum carbon-dated to 1423–45.

CHIOS, BENEDETTO BORDONE

Benedetto Bordone's *Isolario* (*Book of Islands*), published in 1528, helped to popularize a new genre of map collections, those which provided maps of the Mediterranean islands and some further afield. Originally intended as a guide to mariners, with descriptions of the islands and their ports, *isolarii* (as collections of island maps became known) enjoyed a strange flowering in the 15th and 16th centuries before disappearing again. They formed a kind of cross between navigational aid, tourist guide and encyclopaedia, with an air of the exotic that appealed to armchair travellers.

PORTOLAN CHARTS, 1296 ONWARDS

Portolan charts were designed for navigators. They are distinctive in focussing almost entirely on the coast and neglecting the interior, except for flags to indicate territories. This example is from the 16th century. These charts show the sea criss-crossed by rhumb lines, which show the 32 directions of the mariner's compass at a given point. By convention, the eight winds (north, northeast, east, etc.) were drawn in black or brown, the next eight half-winds (north-northeast, etc.) in green, and the 16 quarter winds in red, so that navigators did not have to count round to find their direction. The charts did not take account of the curvature of the Earth and so were of no use for ocean crossings.

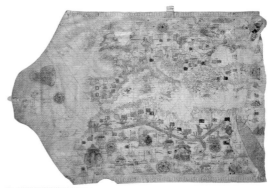

They were usually drawn on sheepskin vellum, making them robust in the salt-water environment. Some still clearly have the shape of the original hide with the thin neck-end of the animal to the west.

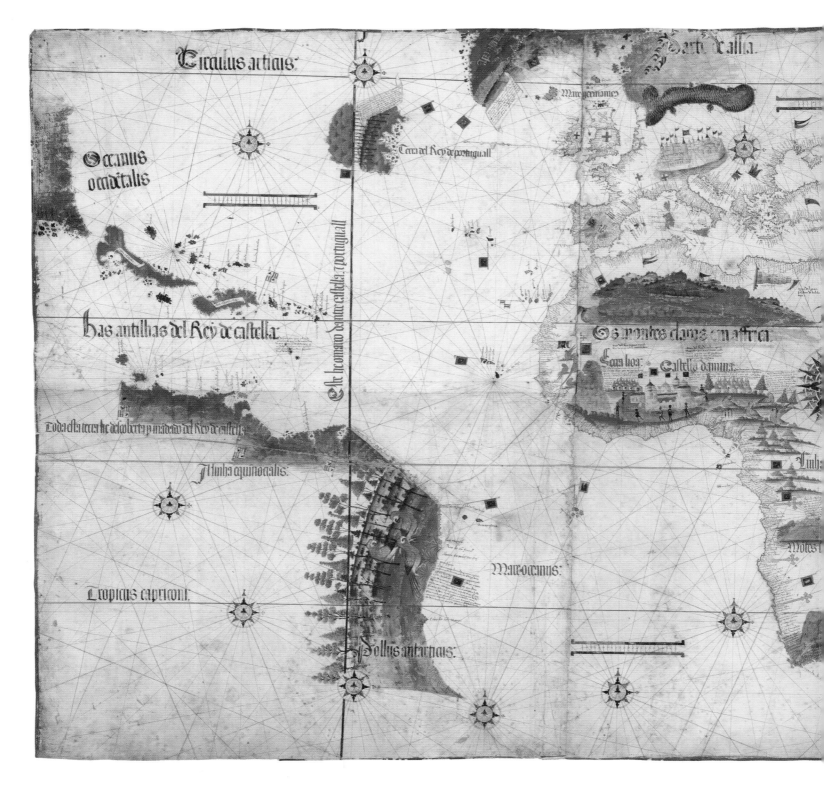

CANTINO PLANISPHERE

The Cantino Planisphere, drawn in 1502, is the earliest surviving map to show parts of the coast of Brazil, discovered in 1500 by the Portuguese explorer Pedro Álvares Cabral. The depiction of the African coast (both sides) is also remarkably accurate. The map is important in that it was acquired for Alfonso d'Este, Duke of Ferrara, in Italy by his agent, Alberto Cantino. The official

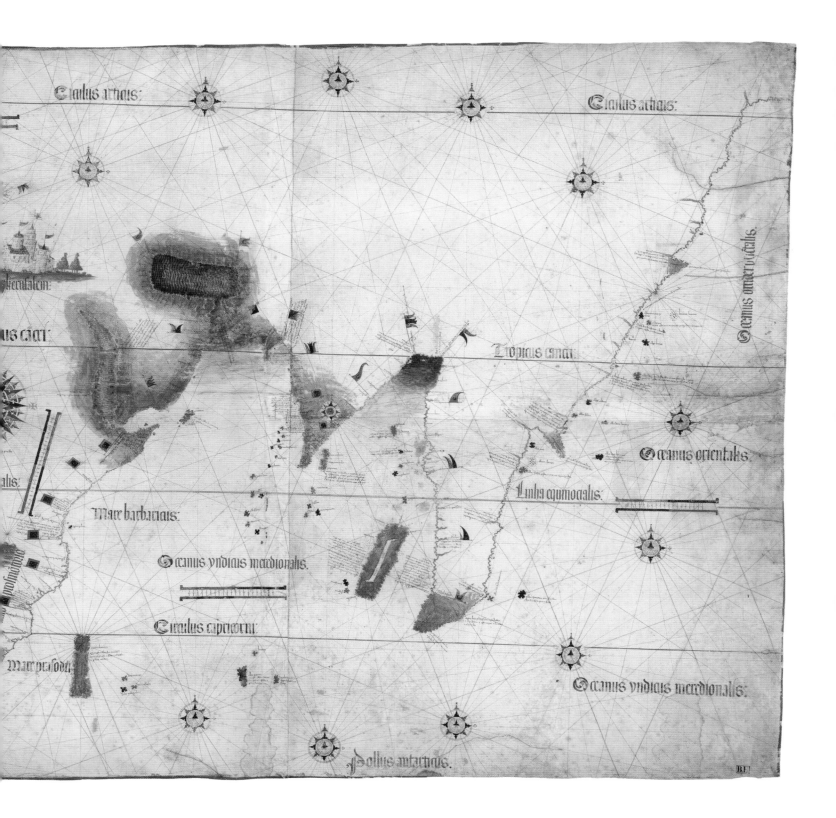

reason for Cantino's visit to Portugal was horse-trading, but it seems the unofficial reason was espionage. He acquired the map illicitly, paying 12 ducats for it (a considerable sum). By means of the map, the Duke had information about the coasts of America and Africa not known to many other European states until later.

MILLER ATLAS

The Miller Atlas was one of the greatest cartographic achievements of the 16th century. Produced by three Portuguese cartographers and a miniaturist, it presents twelve charts covering the North Atlantic, northern Europe, the Azores, Madagascar, the Indian Ocean, Indonesia, the China Sea, the Moluccas, Brazil and the Mediterranean.

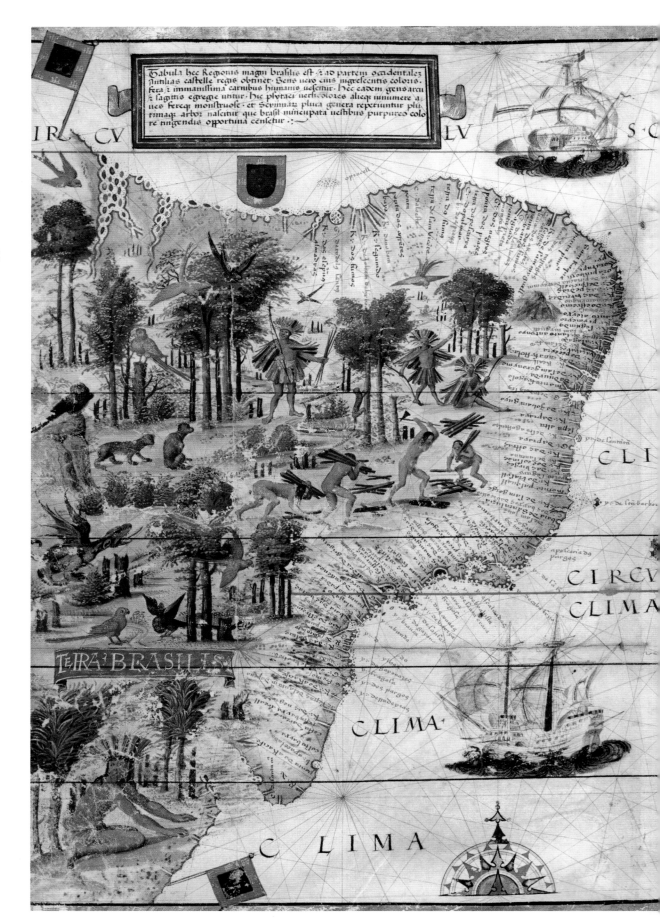

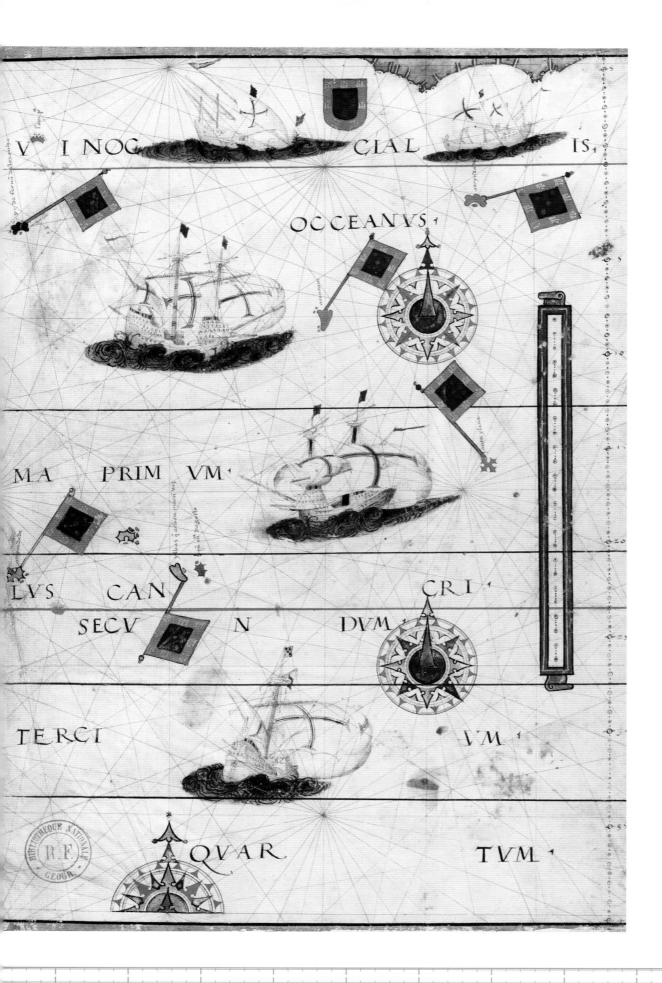

The interior detail exquisitely illustrates what was known of newly discovered lands. The map showing India and Arabia shows the human and animal inhabitants reported by travellers. The map of Brazil (shown here) introduced more detailed topography and better information about the inhabitants than previous maps.

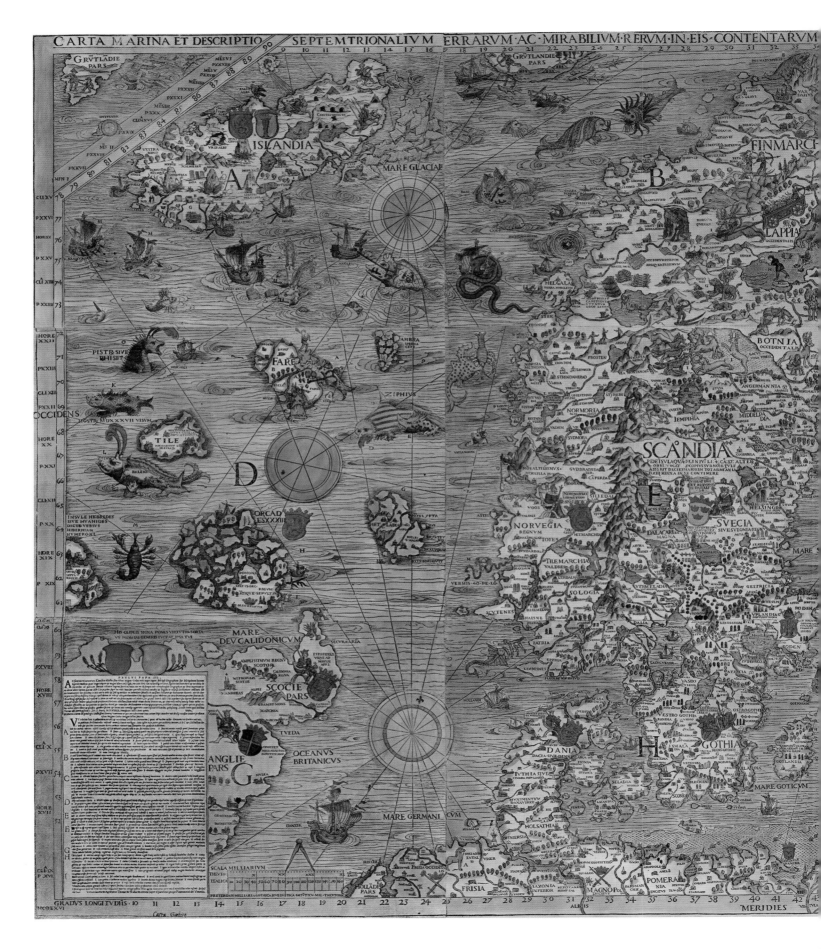

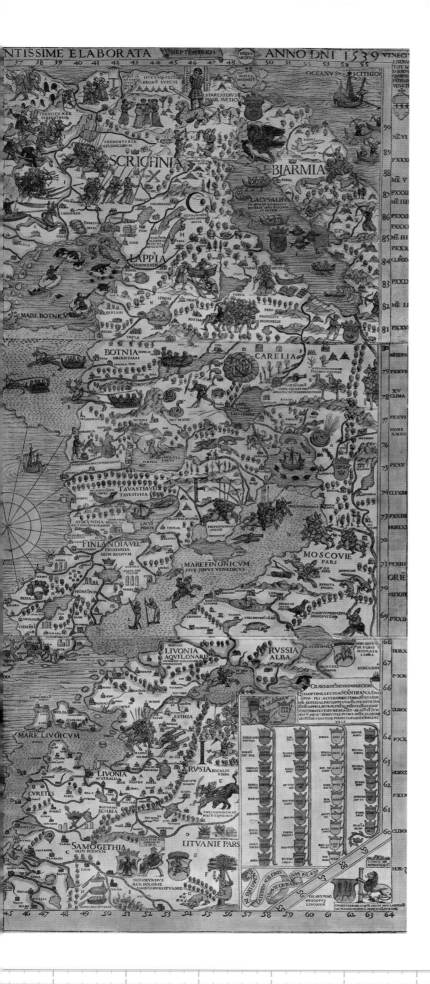

CARTA MARINA

The Carta Marina is the earliest map of the northern countries to give details and place names. It was produced over a period of 12 years by Olaus Magnus, a Swedish writer who lived most of his life outside Sweden. He produced it while living in Poland, and it was printed in Venice from nine woodcut blocks, resulting in a map 1.7 m x 1.25 m (5 ft 6 in x 4 ft). The image is packed with detail of what happens in the lands depicted – such as the tar barrels, dried fish and boat-making shown in Finland. It was the first map to illustrate the sea north of Scandinavia. Volcanoes spewing fire are visible in Iceland.

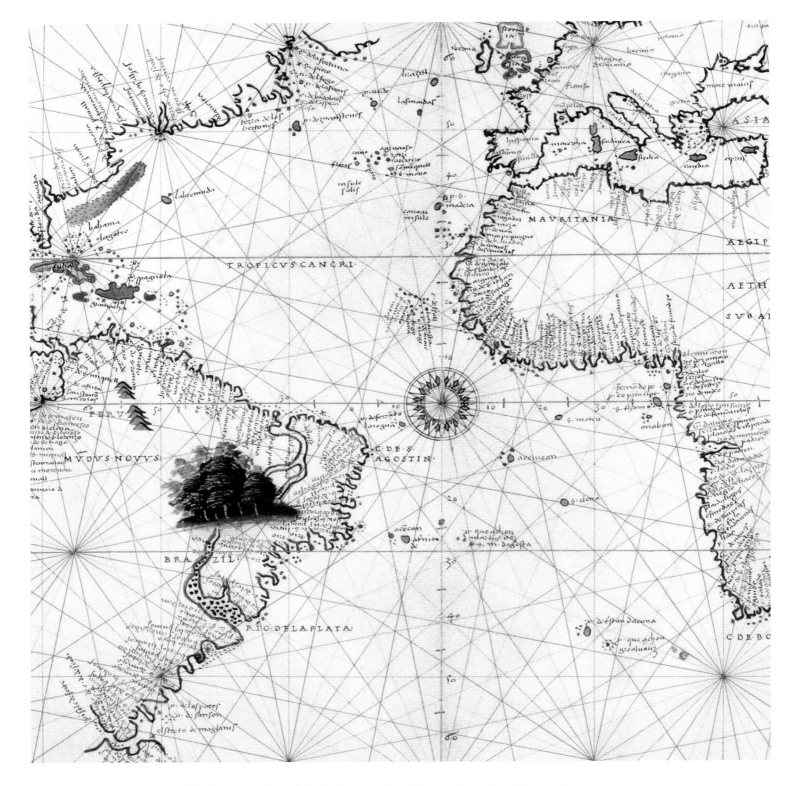

PORTOLAN CHART OF THE ATLANTIC OCEAN

A portolan chart of the Atlantic, showing the coasts of
Europe, North and South America and Africa, as known in
1544. The rhumb lines show how to set a course using the
compass from different locations.

AFRICA, SEBASTIAN MÜNSTER

Sebastian Münster was the first person to print separate maps of the four continents then known: Europe, Africa, Asia and America. In Münster's map of Africa, from 1554, the interior is packed with detail, including mountain ranges (that look like ropes), rivers and some fantastic elements, such as the 'monoculi', a tribe of one-eyed giants. Münster was not an explorer, but a professor of Hebrew – his map was based on descriptions given by scholars and foreigners, and on earlier maps. The geography of the lakes and rivers of Africa is consequently fanciful: the Niger river both begins and ends in lakes, and the Nile starts from two lakes fed by streams from the mythical Mountains of the Moon, retained from Ptolemy's *Geography*. The Sahara Desert is covered by a forest of trees and Madagascar is missed out entirely.

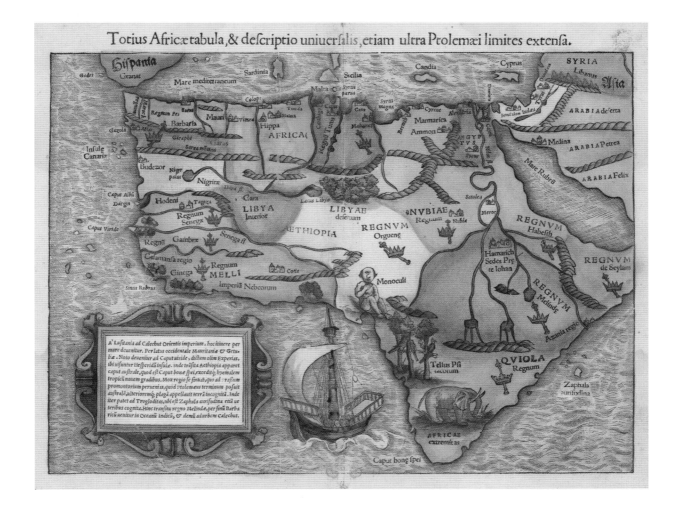

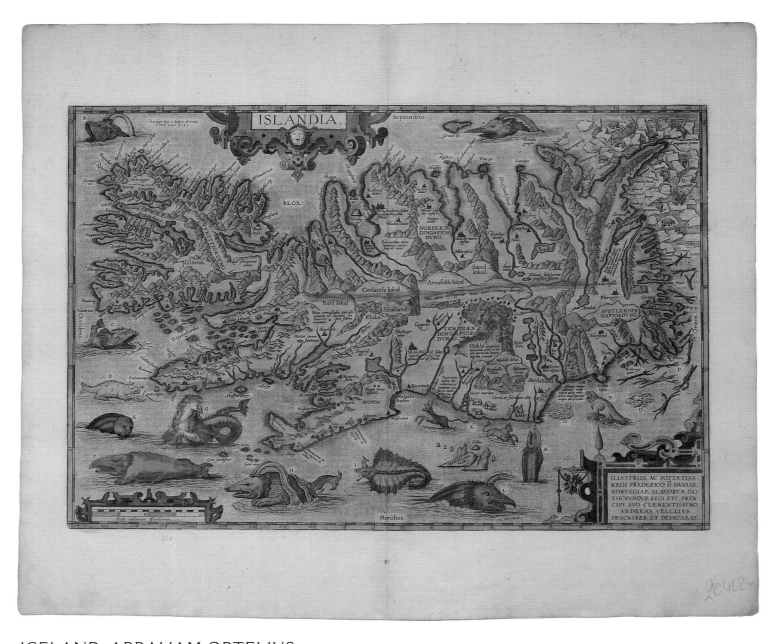

ICELAND, ABRAHAM ORTELIUS

The Flemish cartographer Abraham Ortelius is generally recognized as the author of the first modern atlas. Published in 1570, *Theatrum Orbis Terrarum* contained 53 maps. He added a further 21 maps in later years. Although there were many errors, some of these were corrected in the (many) later editions. Ortelius was the first to comment on the correspondence between the shapes of the African and American coasts, and to suggest a form of continental drift (a theory properly expounded by Alfred Wegener 350 years later in 1912).

Ortelius's map of Iceland is remarkable for the large variety of sea monsters apparently to be found in the area, and recalls the Carta Marina in this and other respects (see pages 94–5).

THE ARCTIC, GERARDUS MERCATOR

Gerardus Mercator's map of the North Pole is the first geographical map of that area. He originally added a small version of it as a vignette to his map of the world (see pages 156–7), recognizing that his new projection made it impossible to show the Pole properly.

Mercator shows the Arctic as a continent split into four equal parts and surrounding a large black rock jutting out of the sea. Contemporary theory held that four rivers rushed towards the Pole, creating a whirlpool that pours water into the interior of the Earth.

NEW FRANCE, MARC LESCARBOT

Marc Lescarbot went on an expedition to Acadia, a colony in Canada, or 'the New France', in 1606–7. He researched the area and its indigenous people extensively, and in 1609 wrote up an account of his travels and discoveries called *Histoire de la Nouvelle-France*. It includes several maps of the area, the first detailed charts of Canadian territory. The map focuses on the coastline and its many inlets, with the interior marked by stylized trees and mountains.

VIRGINIA, JOHN SMITH

John Smith's map of Virginia was created with the assistance of the Algonquins who were more familiar with the land than he was. Smith travelled 2,500 miles around the Chesapeake area in 1607–9. His aims were to explore the region, find riches and seek out a navigable route to the Pacific. The map, drawn for inclusion in Smith's account of Virginia, distinguishes between features that 'hath been discouered' and are marked with crosses, and those known only through the tales of the Algonquin. Smith's astonishingly accurate map remained in use for 70 years. The Algonquins usually drew ephemeral maps for their own use, rather than the permanent records required by Western invaders. They used corn kernels and sticks to make maps on the dirt floors of their huts, so we have no record of Algonquin mapping besides their input to Smith's map.

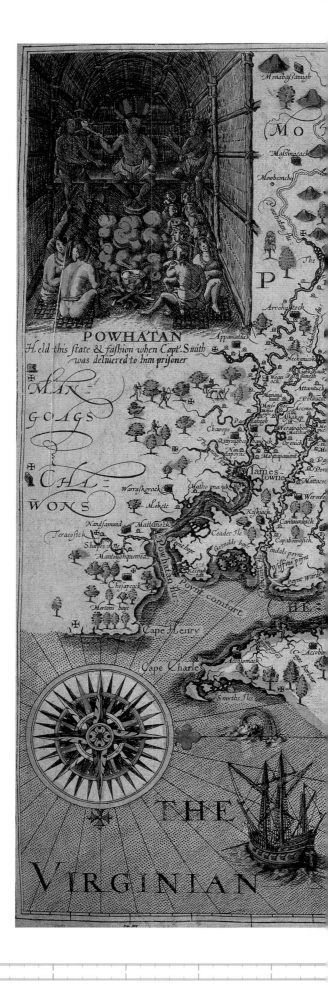

HISPANIOLA AND PUERTO RICO, JOHANNES VINGBOONS

Johannes Vingboons was a Dutch cartographer and watercolourist. His maps were sought after during his lifetime – Queen Christina of Sweden bought 130 of them bound into a three-volume atlas. His map of Hispaniola and Puerto Rico, made in 1639, is possibly the earliest accurate representation of the islands. Vingboons was not a traveller, but researched rigorously and based his maps on the sketches and reports of ships' masters and helmsmen. His collected works represent an accurate record of most of the world known to the Dutch at the time.

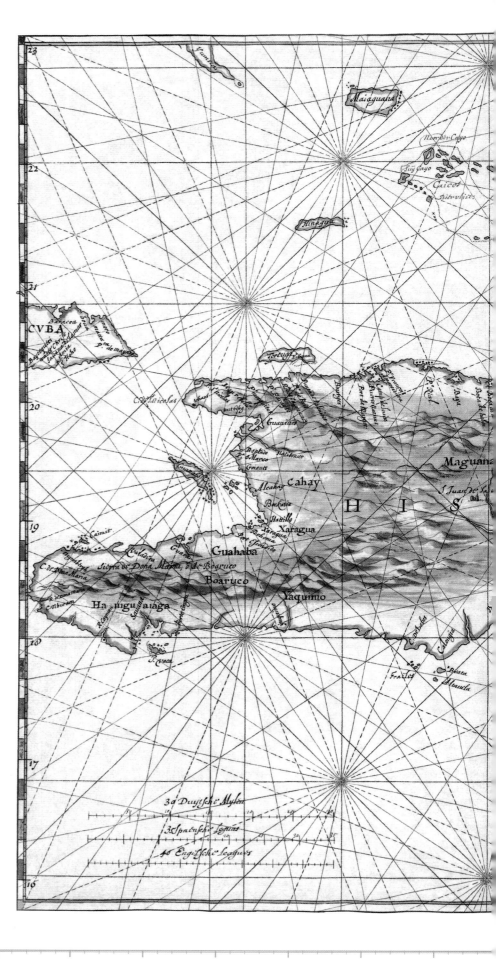

23
22
21
20
19
17
16
Abriojo ó
Cibao pr.
Prov. de la
Vega real
El Cotuy
A N I O L A
Samana
Higuey
C. del Engaño
S. Catalina
Savona
Monica
Mona
I. DE S. IVAN DE P. RICO

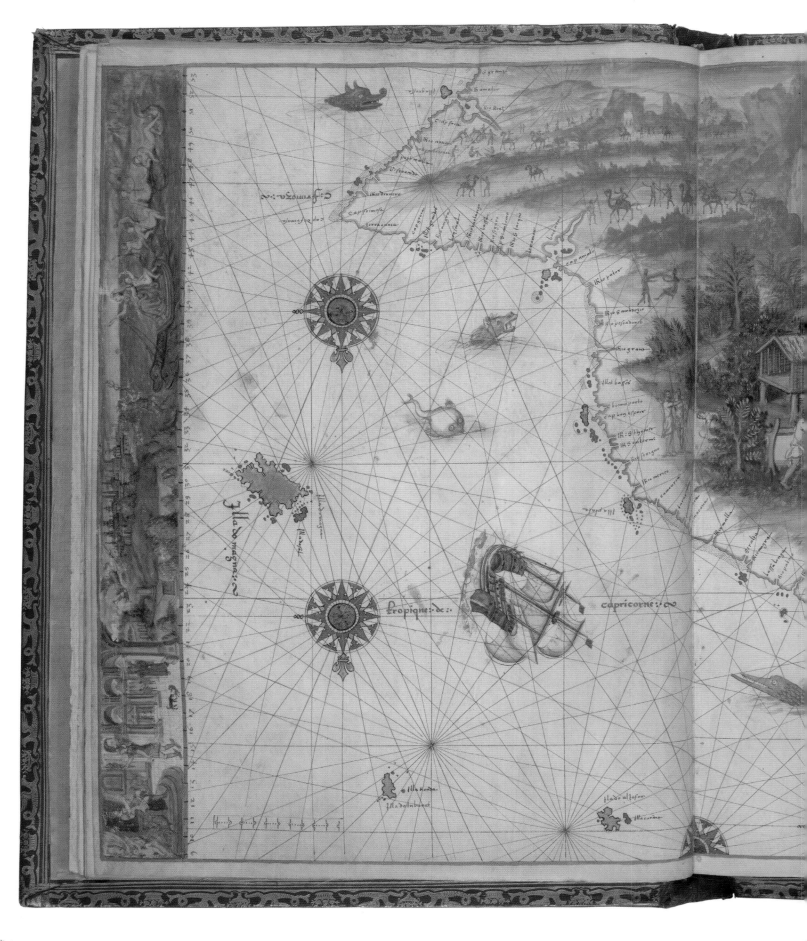

TERRA JAVA

This map of 'Terra Java' from Nicholas Vallard's atlas of 1547 purports to show the east coast of Australia – but Australia was not discovered by Europeans until 1606. There are two possibilities: that the map represents a different landmass, mistaken for Australia, or that the Portuguese really had discovered Australia and kept their discovery secret. That's not as unlikely as it sounds, since a lot of secrecy surrounded exploration at the time. If the Portuguese did really discover Australia so early, their reticence cost them a whole continent.

EAST INDIES, PIETER GOOS

Pieter Goos was a 17th-century Dutch map-maker and engraver. He published a number of nautical maps and sea atlases, all of which aided navigators by including features such as sandbanks and sea depths. His portolan chart of the East Indies was the first map to include Christmas Island, which he labelled 'Mony'. This map was included in his *Zee-Atlas* of 1666. His *Atlas ofte Water-Weereld* (*Atlas or Water World*) is considered one of the best nautical atlases ever produced. His sea charts were used until the 1740s.

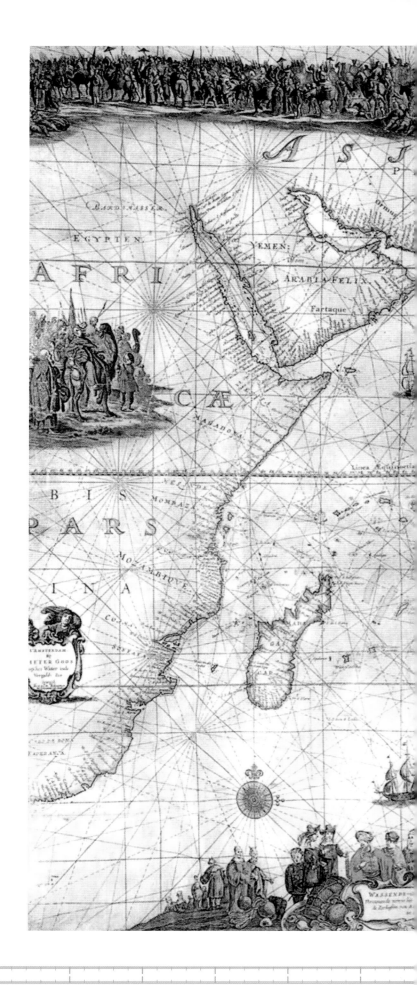

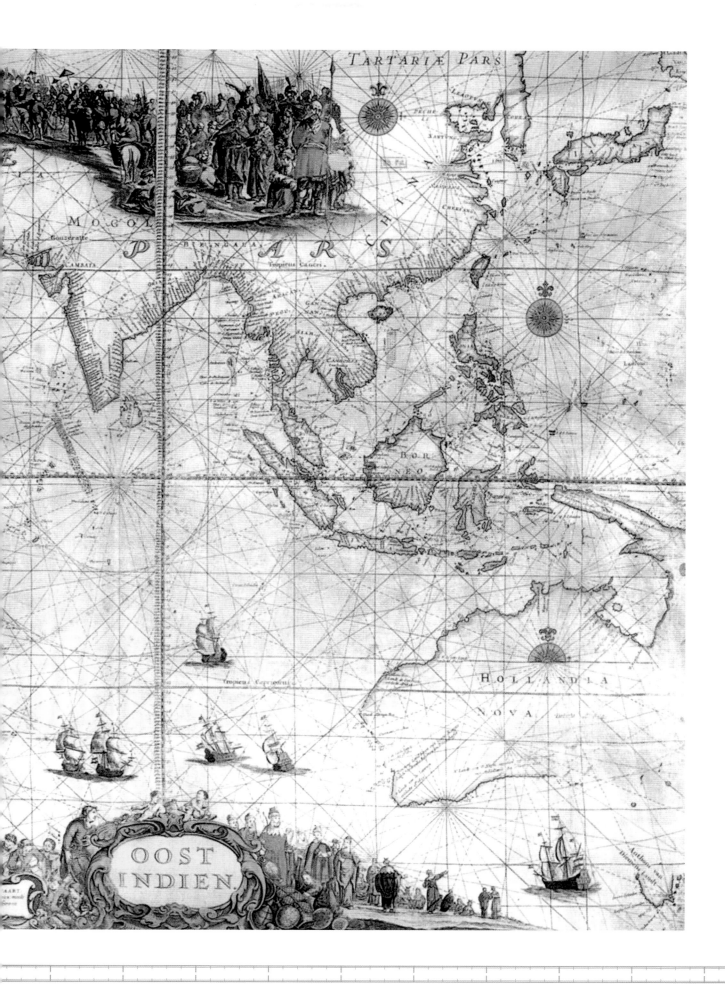

TARTARIÆ PARS

MOGOL

PARS

BORNEO

HOLLANDIA

NOVA

OOST
INDIEN.

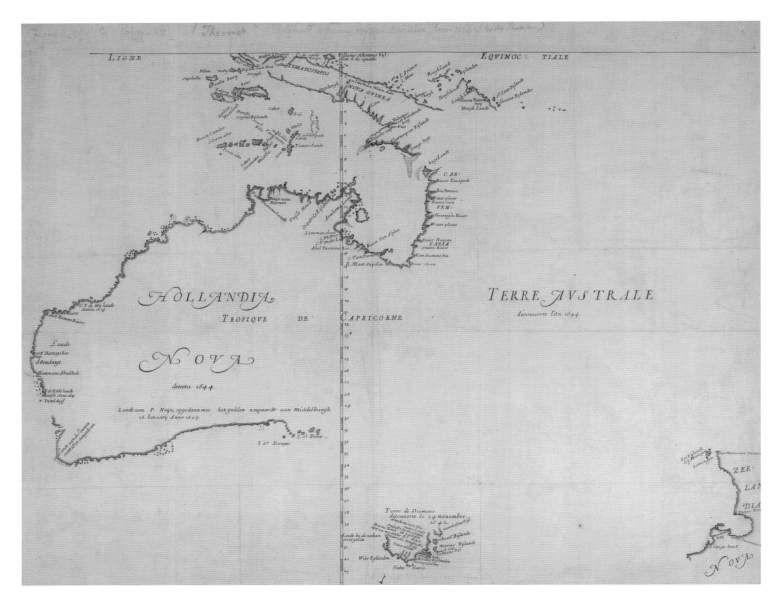

AUSTRALIA, MELCHISÉDECH THÉVENOT

This sketch by Thévenot was drawn following Joan Blaeu's map of Australia, or 'New Holland' as it was known at the time (drawn in 1659, only 53 years after the discovery of Australia by Europeans in 1606). Based on the voyage of Abel Tasman and Willem Jansz, it represents what was known of the coastline – all in the west – but leaves the unexplored interior entirely blank, and large gaps where the coast had not yet been sailed. Tasman's was the fifth European exploratory journey to Australia. Australia was not recognized as a separate continent, rather than part of Asia, until the late 17th century.

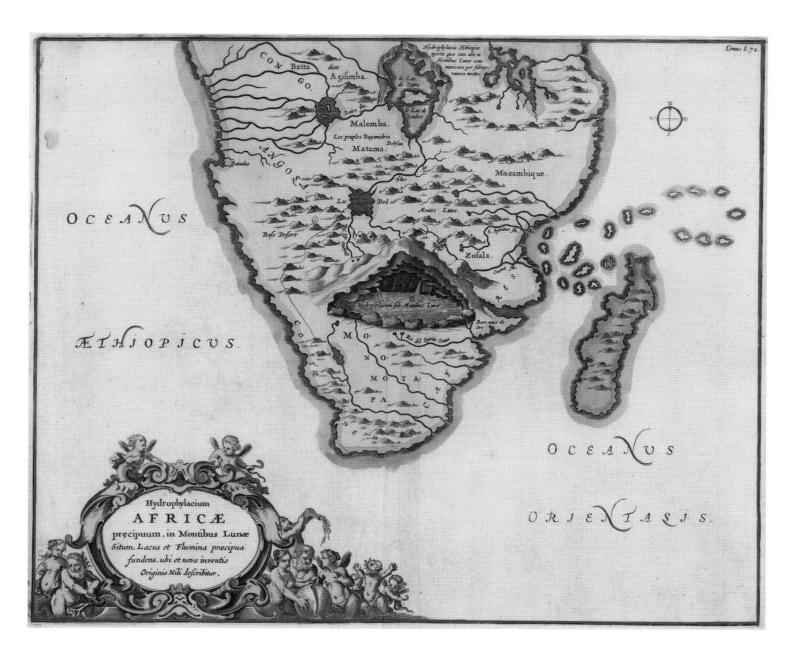

AFRICA, ATHANASIUS KIRCHER

Athanasius Kircher's map of Africa, drawn in 1665, still gives prominence to the mythical Mountains of the Moon, revealing how little was known by European cartographers about the interior of the continent. His map was a visualization of an account told to him by Pedro Páez, a Jesuit colleague, who had visited and described Ethiopia.

Kircher shows the Nile rising from the Mountains of the Moon and flowing through a series of Ethiopian lakes. Although the interior looks quite busy, it is largely filled with stylized mountains, the enormous, mythical source of the Nile, and inaccurate rivers and lakes.

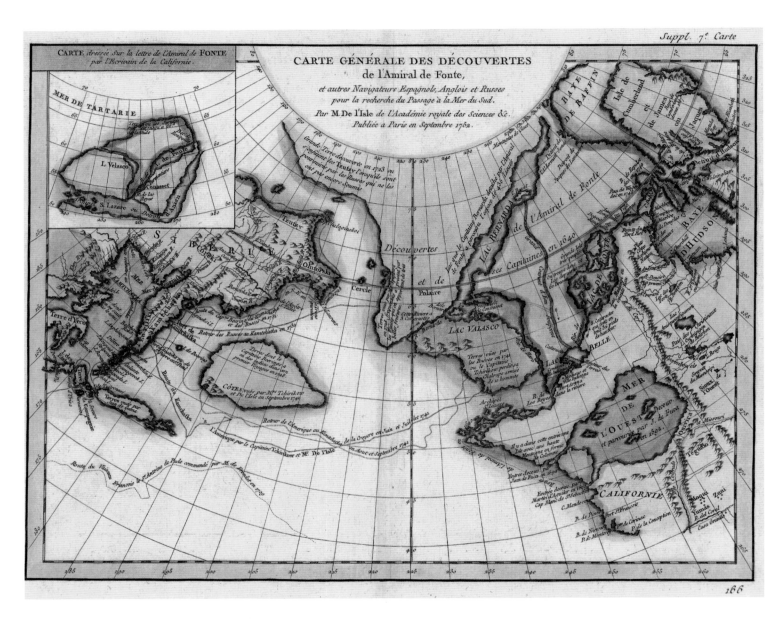

CARTE dressée Sur la lettre de l'Amiral de FONTE
par l'Ecrivain de la Californie.

MER DE TARTARIE

CARTE GÉNÉRALE DES DÉCOUVERTES
de l'Amiral de Fonte,
et autres Navigateurs Espagnols, Anglois et Russes
pour la recherche du Passage à la Mer du Sud.
Par M. De l'Isle de l'Académie royale des Sciences &c.
Publiée à Paris en Septembre 1752.

166

CARTE GENERALE DES DÉCOUVERTES DE L'AMIRAL DE FONTE, JOSEPH-NICOLAS DE L'ISLE

Joseph-Nicolas de l'Isle's map is a strange mix of reality and fantasy. He had spent 21 years in St Petersburg and returned to Paris with unknown and previously secret Russian maps. Working from these, he drew an accurate map of eastern Siberia and the Kamchatka Peninsula. His view of the northwest coast of the Pacific, though, was based on a fictitious account of the voyage of a Spanish admiral, Bartholeme de Fonte, which supposedly took place in 1640. That part of his map bears no relation to the real state of the Pacific coast, as it is entirely made up.

THE RUSSIAN DISCOVERIES, FROM THE MAP PUBLISHED BY THE IMPERIAL ACADEMY OF ST PETERSBURG, ROBERT SAYER

After de l'Isle published his map, the authorities in St Petersburg accused him of stealing the information (quite reasonably, as they were keeping their discoveries secret) and employed a German cartographer, Gerhard Müller, to work in St Petersburg and make an accurate map, correcting the mistakes made by de l'Isle.

Sayer's map is a copy of Müller's officially sanctioned document. Although the Russian territories are depicted accurately, Japan is distorted (and the northern island missing). The outline of North America has been approximated with a dotted outline, but a mythical 'River of the West' is shown as though it were known to exist.

AUSTRALIA, LOUIS DE FREYCINET

The first full map of Australia ever published was the result of Nicholas Baudin's French expedition to the continent in 1800–3, approved by Napoleon. Baudin was the first European to discover parts of the southern coast and all of the western coast. He encountered a British team also mapping the coastline; it's thought that he prepared a report for Napoleon on how to capture the British land-holdings in Australia. The map shows the coastline in detail, but a starkly empty interior, as yet unexplored. The first edition gave new French names to many places already named and discovered. They were corrected later, the original names being reinstated.

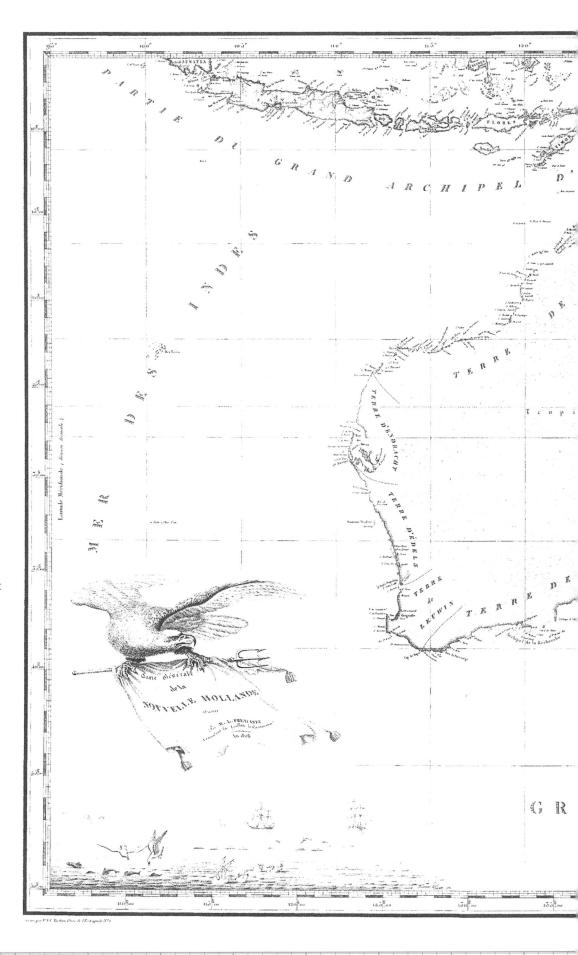

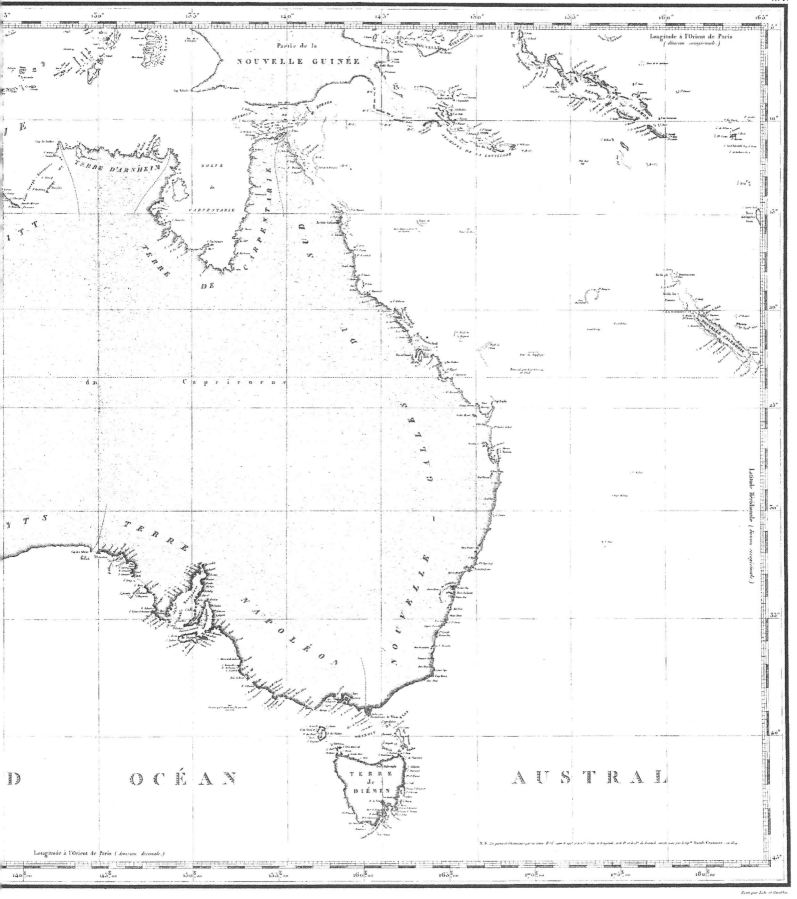

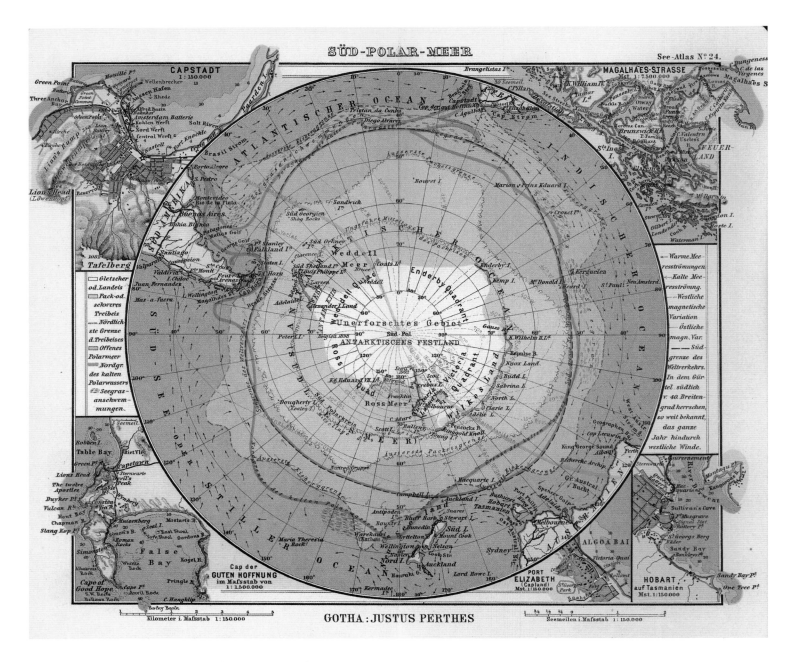

ANTARCTICA, JUSTUS PERTHES

There had long been a belief that a large landmass in the southern hemisphere balanced the lands of the northern hemisphere, and with this in mind some cartographers included a speculative southern continent long before Antarctica had been discovered and charted. This map from 1906, published by the German map-maker Justus Perthes, shows the proper shape of Antarctica.

With no roads or rivers, with most landscape features hidden beneath the snow and the coast obscured by pack ice for much of the year, it was a difficult challenge for cartographers. More detailed mapping of Antarctica was not possible until the use of seismic data and aerial photography in the second half of the 20th century.

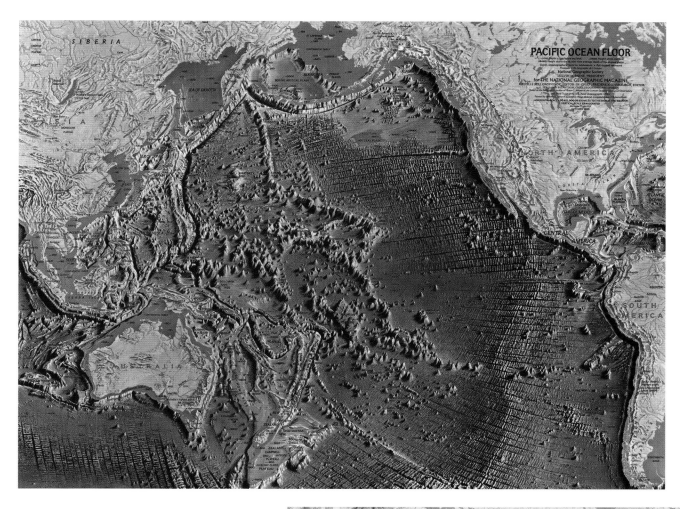

SEABED

There was no substantial mass of dry land left to discover by the end of the 19th century, though there was still some refining of coastlines to be achieved. In the 20th century, exploration turned instead to the seabed and to the moon and other planets.

These maps, achieved with the use of satellite technology, show that mountain ranges and plains are found not only on land but also far beneath the ocean. The Pacific in the area of Asia and Australia is particularly rich in seabed features, with towering mountains and the plunging depths of the Mariana Trench (the dark curved line below Japan). Reaching a depth of 11 km (6.8 miles), it is the deepest canyon on Earth.

CHAPTER 4

WORLD VISIONS

The map of the world has grown over the centuries as people have travelled further afield.

LONG AGO, PEOPLE ONLY KNEW the area they could cover on foot or by river. The earliest world maps reflect this, showing the small, known world at the centre and then drifting into fantasy for the unknown areas. For well over 1,000 years, the European world view was modelled on the theories of the geographer Ptolemy. Then, from the 15th century, new lands were added to the globe: first the Americas, then southern parts of Africa, Asia, the Pacific Islands and Australasia, and finally Antarctica. The world became unmanageably large for the existing models. Three new map styles emerged: east and west hemispheres, each in their own circular map; the globe unrolled as a rectangular or oval map; or a number of geometrical segments, called gores, which could be pasted onto a sphere. Representing a sphere's surface on a flat page brings inevitable distortion. The challenge presented by this led to the development of new projections, attempting to minimize the distortion. The world as we perceive it today is defined by these projections.

1 'Mountain'
2 'City'
3 Assyria
4 Swamp
5 Canal
6 'City'
7 Babylon divided
  by Euphrates
8 Ocean (salt water)

IMAGO MUNDI

This world map drawn on a Babylonian clay tablet 2,600 years ago is possibly the oldest non-mythological depiction of the world. It places Babylon at the centre of a round world surrounded by water labelled a river of 'bitter water'. There are seven islands in this surrounding sea. It seems to show, in the central Earth, a mountain, several cities, rivers and a swamp. The shape of the world known to the Babylonians might have influenced the medieval T-O maps (see page 123).

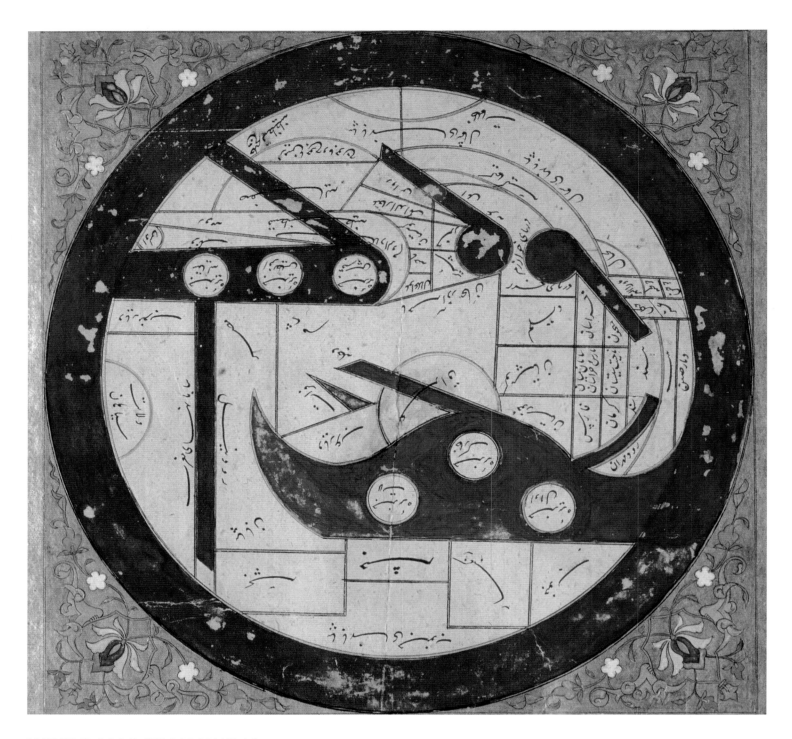

WORLD MAP, IBN HAWQAL

Drawn in the Balkhi school (see page 22) around 977, Ibn Hawqal's 'wheel map' of the world is highly stylized. It shows the world known to Islam at the time of its composition, surrounded by an ocean. It is oriented with east at the top. The larger interior body of water is the Indian Ocean, with the Arab peninsula jutting out into it. The smaller body of water is the Mediterranean Sea. Ibn Hawqal was

a contemporary of al-Istakhri, and they exchanged and corrected each other's maps. Ibn Hawqal wrote extensive commentaries on the places shown in his book of maps, which followed the standard format for an Islamic atlas with a world map, charts of three seas (the Mediterranean, the Persian Gulf and the Caspian) and 17 maps of separate Islamic countries.

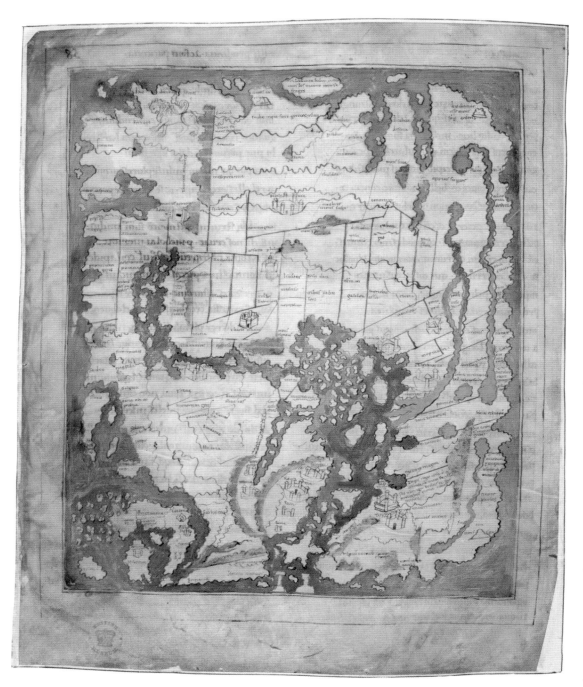

The Anglo-Saxon world map, or mappa mundi, contains the earliest known relatively accurate depiction of the British Isles. It was created between 1025 and 1050, probably in Canterbury, with the most recent information included dating from around 1000. East is at the top of the map, and the British Isles are in the bottom left-hand corner. London, Winchester and Dublin are indicated using Roman-style town symbols.

The map does not belong to any of the established or emerging traditions of map-making, such as the T-O maps (see page 123), the Ptolemaic maps (pages 124–5) or the Beatus tradition (pages 122–3). Its detailed depiction of coastlines would not be matched before the portolan charts of the later Middle Ages.

Northwest Europe is depicted quite well, but the Mediterranean countries are distorted. To the east, the map extends as far as the Red Sea and the Persian Gulf. Asia is shown at right angles to the coast of North Africa. The map shows the settlement places of the Twelve Tribes of Israel and that might have been part of its function.

SAINT-SEVER BEATUS

The Saint-Sever Beatus is the best executed and most representative of the maps made in the Beatus tradition (so called because they appear in a commentary on the Book of Revelation written by Saint Beatus of Liébana). It was made around 1050. It shows 270 named features and more rivers than any other version. East is at the top; to the right, the Red Sea cuts off Africa, Arabia and India and beyond it lie the 'antipodes'. While Europe and Africa have cities, denoted by castles, the area of the antipodes is packed with text describing its legendary inhabitants. The monastery of Saint-Sever (the church in the lower left quadrant) is given as much prominence as Rome and Constantinople. Jerusalem is – unusually – not especially distinguished. The sausage-shaped island in the lower left border is Britain.

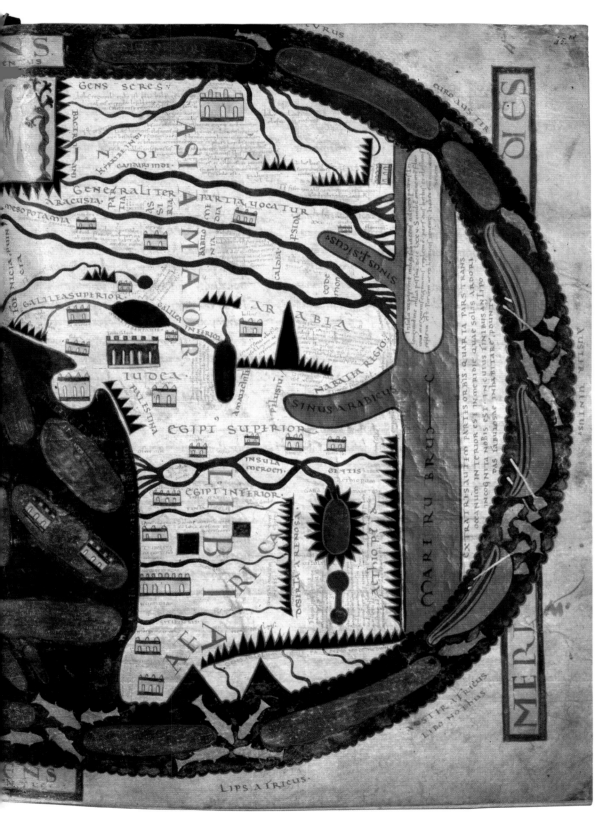

T-O MAP

The Beatus maps follow the T-O model in which a stylized circular world is shown divided by a T shape, with Asia at the top (in the east) and the lower portion split into Europe and Africa.

PTOLEMAIC MAP OF THE INHABITED WORLD

Ptolemy's writings on geography were the most influential source for European and Middle-Eastern map-makers for many centuries, though the oldest surviving copies were written around 1,000 years after his death. If Ptolemy actually drew any maps, they have been lost, but he set out a cartographic method, relating locations to a grid that approximates latitude/longitude. He was the first to apply mathematics to the problem of representing the surface of the spherical Earth on a flat document.

Maps drawn from Ptolemy's descriptions and instructions show the inhabited world as far as he knew it. Nothing was known of the southern parts of Africa, north Asia, the Americas, Australasia, Antarctica, the most northerly parts of Europe and Russia, or of the Pacific and Atlantic Oceans. This 13th-century Byzantine reconstruction follows Ptolemy's instructions for map-making. Ptolemy's work only became widely known in Europe from the 15th century.

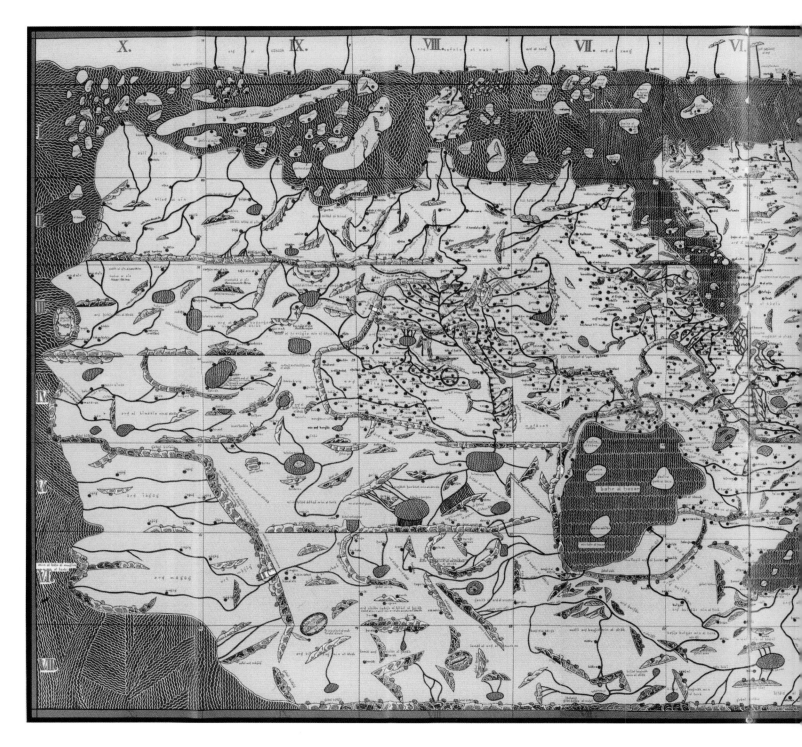

TABULA ROGERIANA, AL-IDRISI

Dissatisfied with the inaccuracies of existing maps, Roger II of Sicily charged the Arab geographer Muhammad al-Idrisi with compiling a new, accurate world atlas taking the best information available. It took 15 years to complete, during which time al-Idrisi and his colleagues interviewed many travellers, rigorously testing all knowledge they were given. Al-Idrisi divided the world into seven climates, following Ptolemy, then split each into ten, creating a total of 70 maps and descriptive

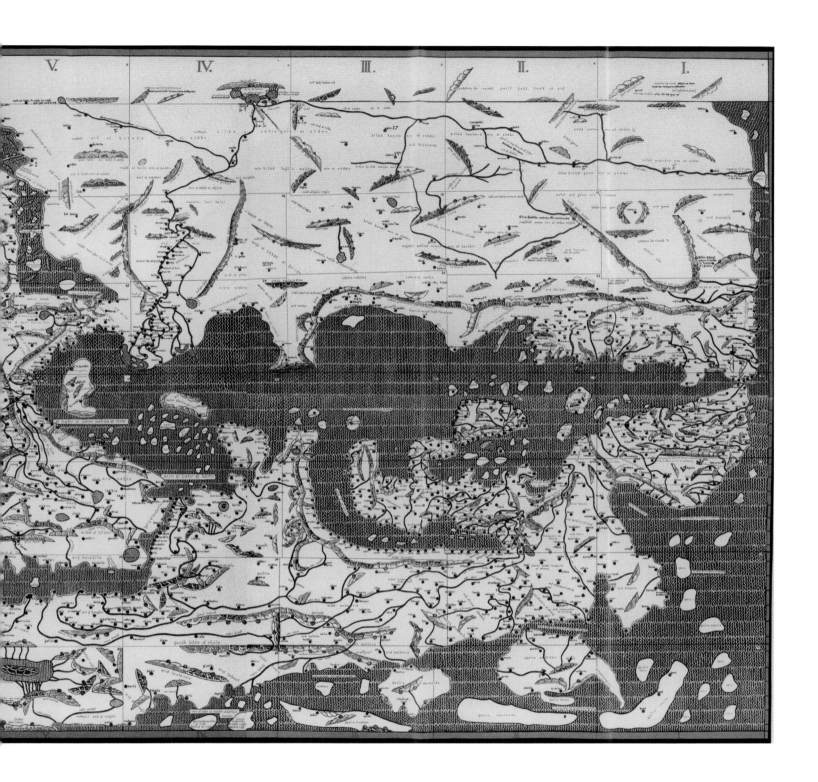

accounts. The book was completed in 1154, a few weeks before Roger's death. The map as shown here is a compilation of the maps in the book, oriented with south at the top. Africa continues along the top margin and under the Indian Ocean.

The Mediterranean is in the lower half of the right-hand side. The Tabula Rogeriana, or Kitab Rujar, remained the most accurate world map for 300 years.

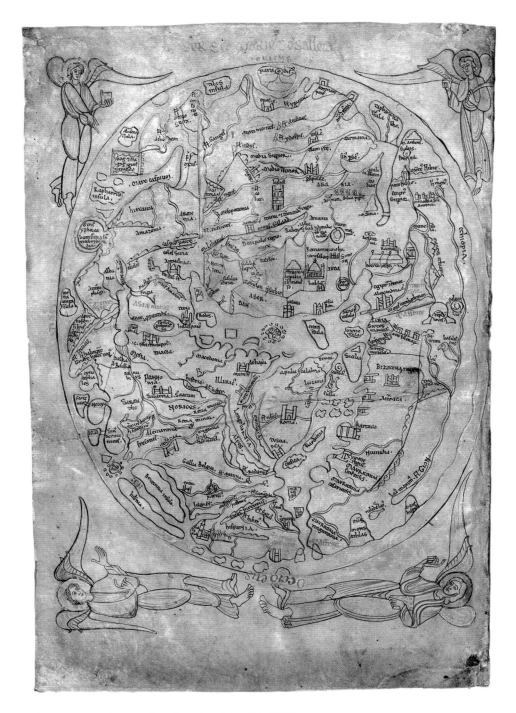

SAWLEY MAP, HONORIUS AUGUSTODUNENSIS

This world map was drawn by the 12th-century monk and theologian Honorius Augustodunensis (d. 1154) who lived for some time in Germany and for some time in Britain. Known as the Sawley map, it was included in the *Imago Mundi*, an encyclopaedia of world history, geography and cosmology. It draws on blended classical and Christian traditions. The Mediterranean is placed at the centre of the map (rather than Jerusalem which is central in later medieval mappae mundi). The places marked include existing cities of the 12th century and mythical locations, including Paradise at the top. Scylla and Charybdis are represented by a dog's head and a spiral near the island of Sicily. The British Isles are at the lower left and Africa to the right. It's likely that the Hereford Mappa Mundi (see page 130) drew on the Sawley map.

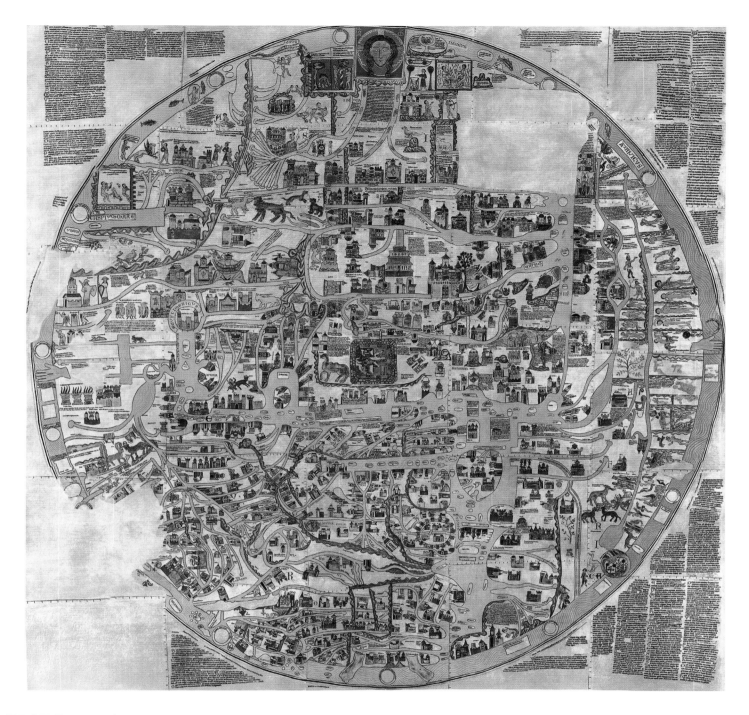

EBSTORF MAP

The largest of all medieval world maps, the 13th-century Ebstorf map was drawn on 30 pieces of goatskin sewn together to create a single sheet 3.5 m (11½ ft) square. The original was destroyed by Allied bombs in World War II, but it has been recreated from surviving photographs. The map shows the known world within the body of Christ, with his head at the top (east), hands to either side and feet at the bottom. Jerusalem is in the centre, showing a scene of the Crucifixion. The map is packed with detail – a total of 2,345 entries comprising 1,500 pieces of text and 845 pictures, including geographical locations, mythical beasts or tribes and Bible references.

HEREFORD MAPPA MUNDI, RICHARD DE BELLO

Created around 1290, the Hereford Mappa Mundi is one of the finest surviving. It is drawn on a single sheet of vellum (calfskin) and, with the central circle 1.3 m (4 ft 3 in) across, it is the largest surviving medieval map. It puts Jerusalem at the centre of the world, which is oriented with east at the top. Drawing on a host of sources for its information, it presents not just (or even especially) geographical information, but a wealth of social, mythological and religious detail. Unusually for a medieval map, it names its creator – Richard of Haldingham and Lafford, who has been identified as Richard de Bello.

WORLD MAP, PIETRO VESCONTE

Pietro Vesconte was one of the first cartographers to name and date his maps; this world map dates from 1321. He also demonstrated greater interest in geographical accuracy than his predecessors. Outside his own areas of experience, though, he still relied on sources that were far less accurate, so Africa, east Asia and the northern regions are as distorted as ever. He has dropped most of the mythological content, but retains the mythical figure of Prester John, a Christian ruler supposedly living in a lost eastern or African nation. Here John is shown near the coast of India at the top right, labelled 'Fre Judig' (Frère John).

CATALAN WORLD MAP

Attributed to the Jewish illuminator Cresques Abraham, the Catalan Atlas from 1375 is the best-preserved map drawn by the Majorcan school of cartographers in the Middle Ages. It comprises six vellum leaves, originally folded but now cut down the middle, mounted on wooden boards.

The map was created at a time when a loose confederate of Aragon states dominated seagoing in the Mediterranean. The Aragonese thalassocracy (maritime kingdom) consisted of many islands, including the Balearics, Sardinia, Sicily and some Greek islands. The atlas, commissioned by Catalan Aragon rulers, is in part a celebration and tool of imperial pride. It combines elements of the portolan charts with interior detail, much of it (in the eastern portion) drawn from travellers' tales, such as those of John Mandeville and Marco Polo. The political allegiance of cities is shown by a flag.

WORLD MAP, GIOVANNI LEARDO

Probably produced in 1452 or 1453, Giovanni Leardo's mappa mundi is labelled in Venetian dialect, with east at the top. In the north (on the left) there is a 'desert uninhabited due to cold', and in the south (right), a 'desert uninhabited due to heat'. Following a common tradition, Leardo included Paradise at the top (blurred as a result of damage to the map) and Mount Sinai and Mount Ararat, the latter with Noah's ark stranded on it.

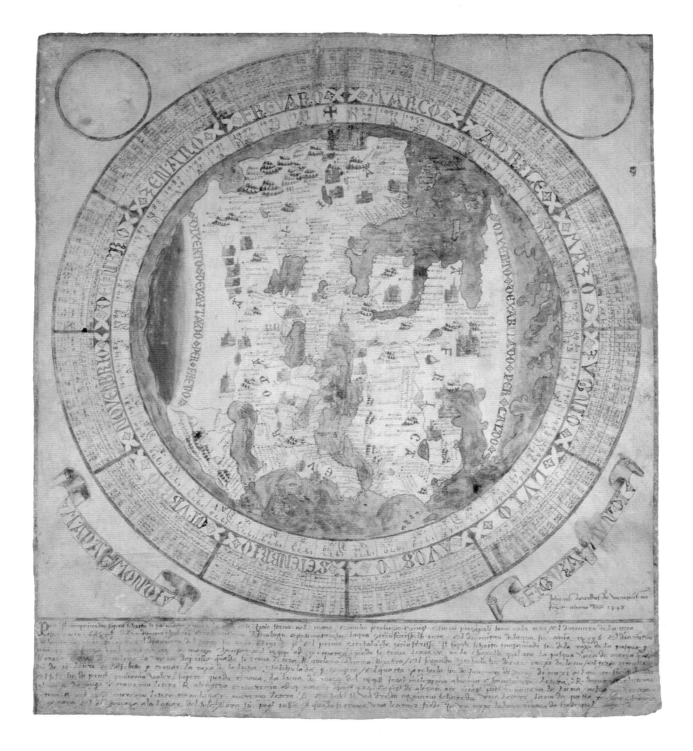

WORLD MAP, FRA MAURO

Fra Mauro's map, made in Venice in 1450, has been called the last medieval mappa mundi. It does reflect the encyclopaedic concerns of the mappae mundi, with numerous illustrations and annotations, but Fra Mauro steps beyond the Middle Ages in criticizing Ptolemy. He includes places that were not known to Ptolemy, following Ptolemy's approach rather than his specific model, and excuses this in a note on the map. South is at the top, following the Islamic tradition (Ptolemy put north at the top). It is one of the first Western maps to show Japan, with an island below Java labelled 'Cimpagau'. The map is two metres across, drawn on parchment and set in a wooden frame.

GENOESE WORLD MAP, 1457

This beautiful map on vellum, created in 1457, combines different map-making traditions in its attempt to incorporate new discoveries and traditions with old. The depiction of the Mediterranean region, most familiar to the map-maker, follows the pattern of the portolan charts, with extensive coastal detail and rhumb lines. Further afield, the influence of the Ptolemaic tradition and the Arab maps is more prominent. Although southern Africa is distorted, Ethiopia liberally sprinkled with dragons and India underdeveloped, there is a clear attempt at accurate rather than mythical representation.

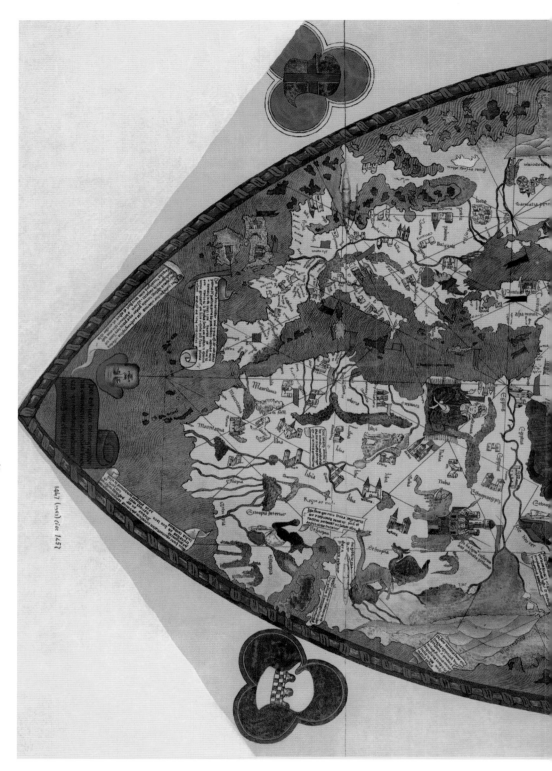

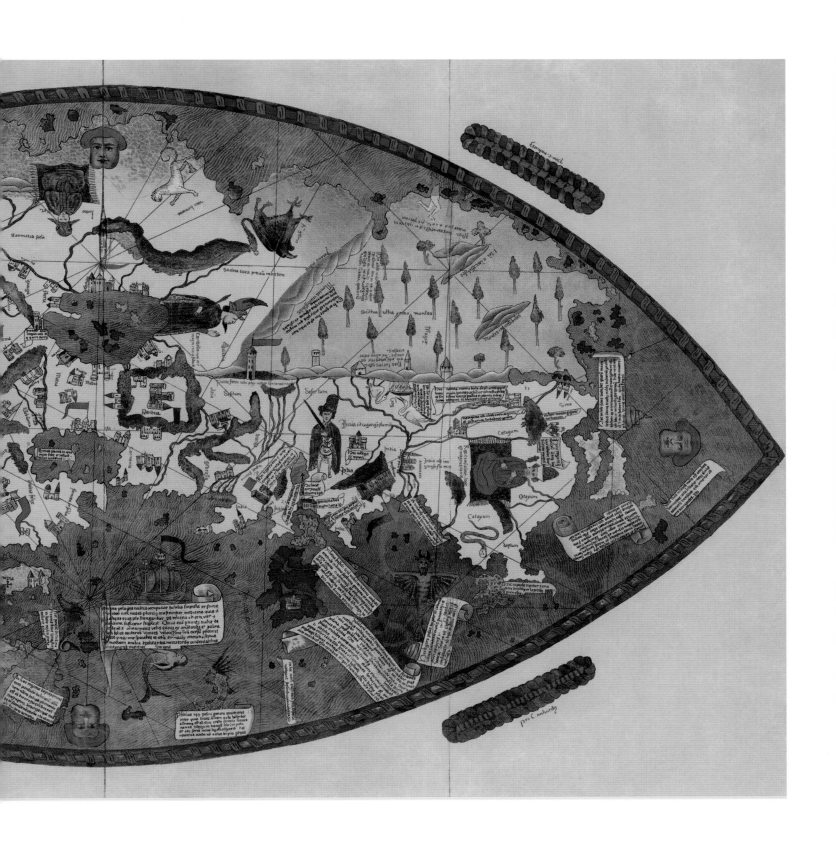

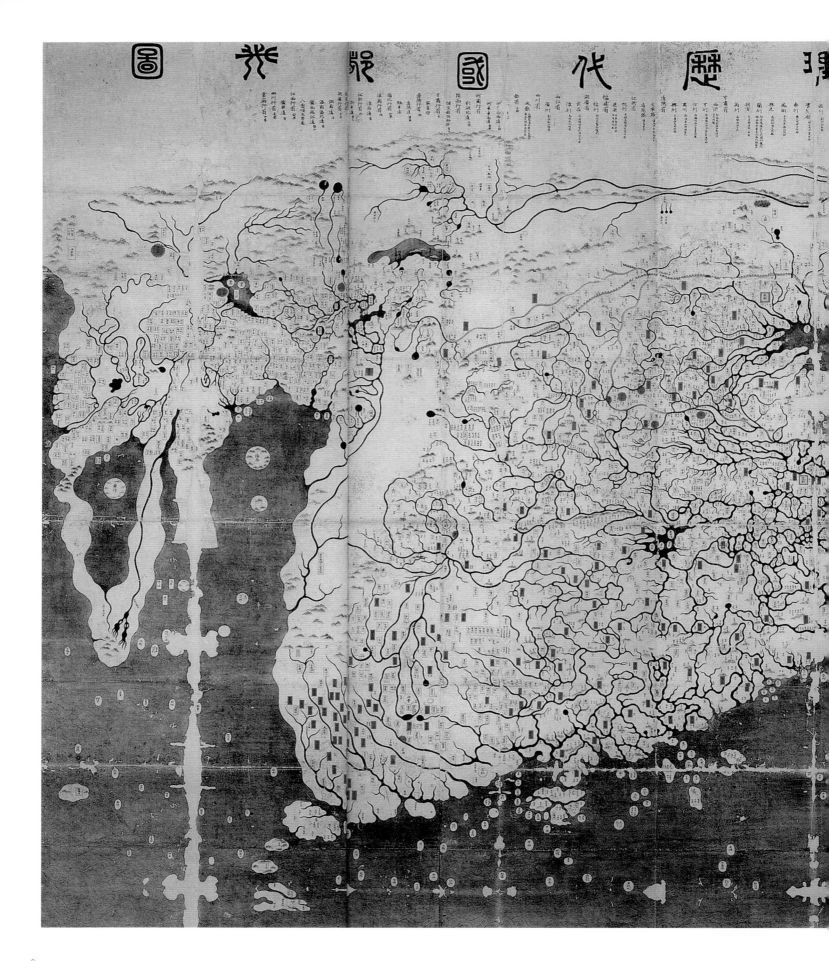

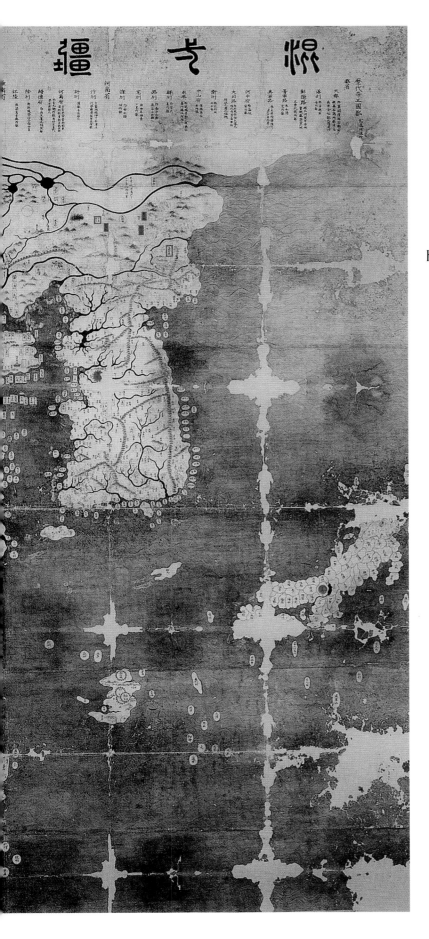

KANGNIDO

Painted on stiff silk in Korea in 1470, the Honil Gangni Yeokdae Gukdo Ji Do ('Map of Integrated Lands and Regions of Historical Countries and Capitals'), or Kangnido, is based on a similar map introduced to Korea from Japan in 1402. It is one of the earliest world maps to have survived from southeast Asia.

Japan, although accurate in itself, is wrongly positioned and oriented, having been turned through 90 degrees. The shape (though not the interior) of southern Africa, on the extreme left of the map, is more accurate than in European maps of the same date and probably owes its precision to Arab cartographers. The western bulge of North Africa, though, is missing. All the western lands are disproportionately small, and information on them is of an earlier date. Far Eastern knowledge about Europe was not updated until the 16th and 17th centuries.

MARTELLUS WORLD MAP

Created by the talented German map-maker Henricus Martellus in 1490, this world map linked medieval cartography with the new models of the Renaissance. Like the Genoese world map (pages 136–7), its depiction of the Mediterranean is based on the portolan charts, but further afield it relies on Ptolemy, augmented with new discoveries.

It was the first map to show Africa as described by Bartholomew Diaz after his journey around the Cape of Good Hope in 1487–8. Text recently revealed by multispectral imaging includes information on the interior of Africa probably drawn from an African delegation visiting Italy in 1441, representing the most complete early collection of African geographic information gathered by Africans. The coast of southeast Asia, though, is still hypothetic – that is, totally made up. The Martellus map is thought to have inspired both Martin Behaim's globe of 1492 (page 142) and Columbus's attempt to reach the East by sailing west. Calculations from this map suggest a distance of only 7,200 km (4,474 miles) travelling west, while a journey to India, skirting the artificially elongated Africa, would be 24,000 km (14,913 miles). It appears Africa might have been extended into the frame to make it larger for political purposes – perhaps to support Columbus's petition to sail west.

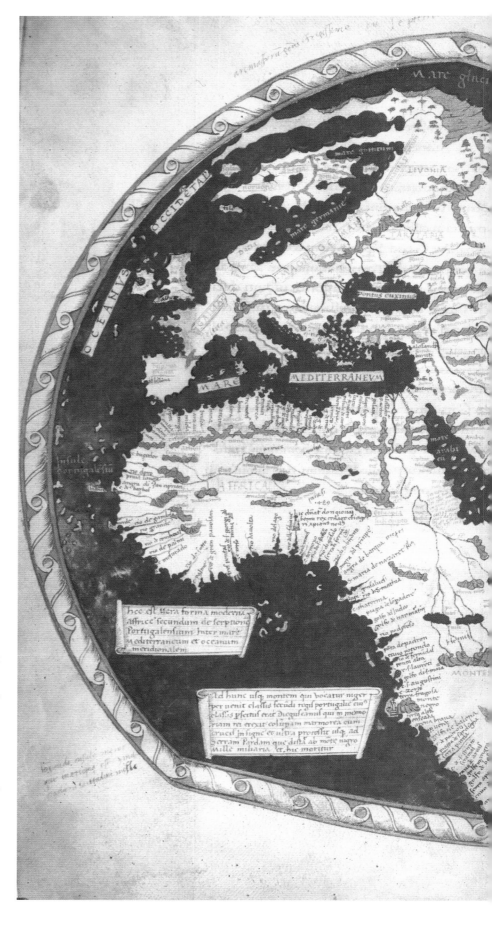

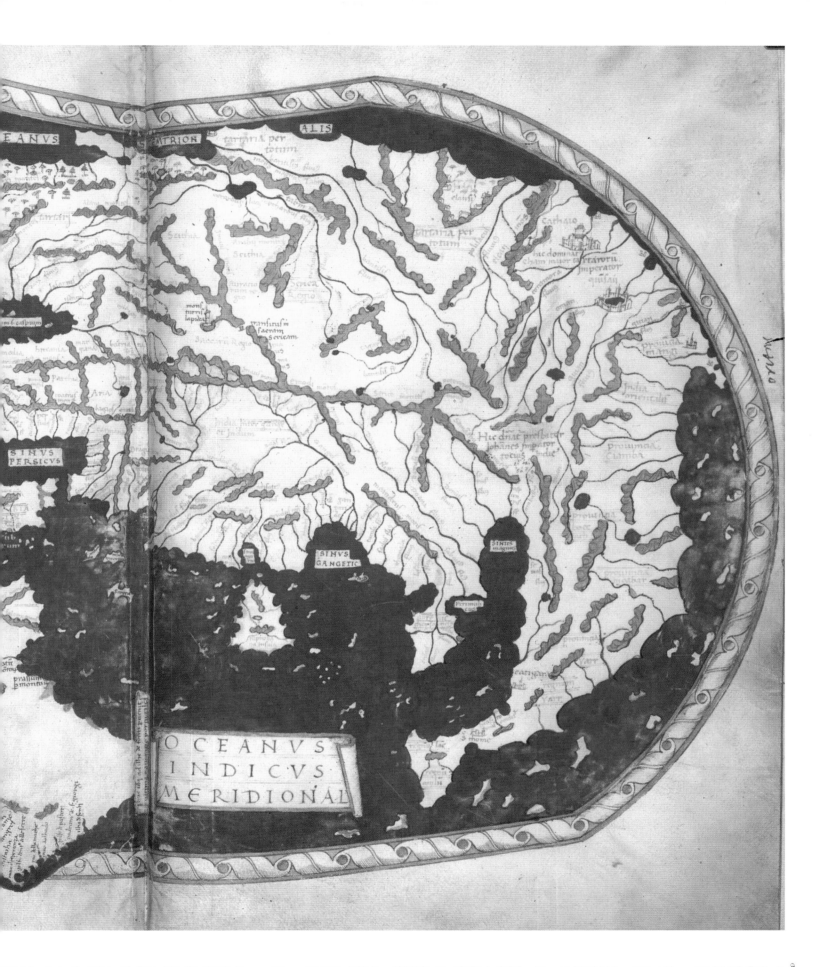

ERDAPFEL, MARTIN BEHAIM

The earliest surviving terrestrial globe was made by the German Martin Behaim in 1492, before the European discovery of the Americas. It is based on Ptolemy's geography, augmented with new discoveries. Besides the topographical information, the surface is packed with additional details drawn from the accounts of travellers (such as Marco Polo) and the great encyclopaedists (such as Isidore of Seville). In the form of annotations and illustrations, it gives details of lands, peoples, beasts (mythological and real), superstitions, legends and natural resources. The single ocean that separates Europe from Asia makes it a short hop of 2,400 km (1,491 miles) to Japan.

OSTRICH-EGG GLOBE

The oldest surviving globe to show the New World was drawn on an ostrich egg in 1504. It is made of the bottom halves of two different ostrich eggs and served as the model for the Hunt-Lenox Globe in the New York Public Library, made of copper alloy and dated 1504–6. It is also the first known map to use the legend 'Hic sunt dracones' – 'here be dragons'. While it shows South America as a sizeable landmass, labelled Mundus Novus (New World), North America is represented by just two small islands. It seems likely that the Hunt-Lenox Globe was cast from the ostrich-egg globe.

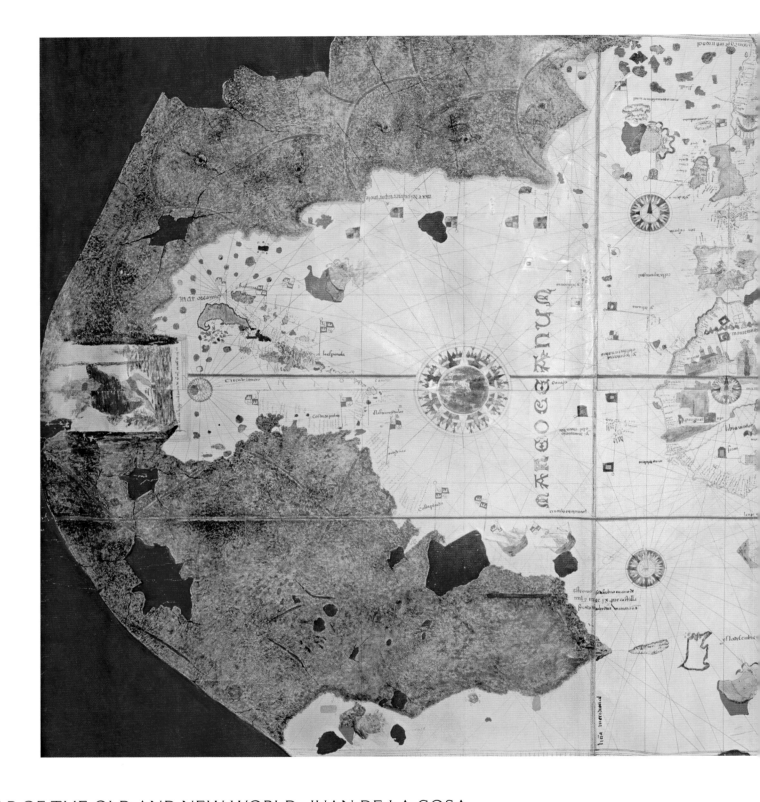

MAP OF THE OLD AND NEW WORLD, JUAN DE LA COSA

This is the earliest surviving map to show the coast of America. Made in 1500 by Juan de la Cosa, who sailed with Columbus, it existed only in manuscript form and no copy was made and published, so it had little influence on mapping traditions.

The map is in fact two maps, one of the Old World and one of the New (de Cosa probably drew only the New World map). It is a portolan chart, showing the coast of North and South America as discovered by sailing along it. The scale of

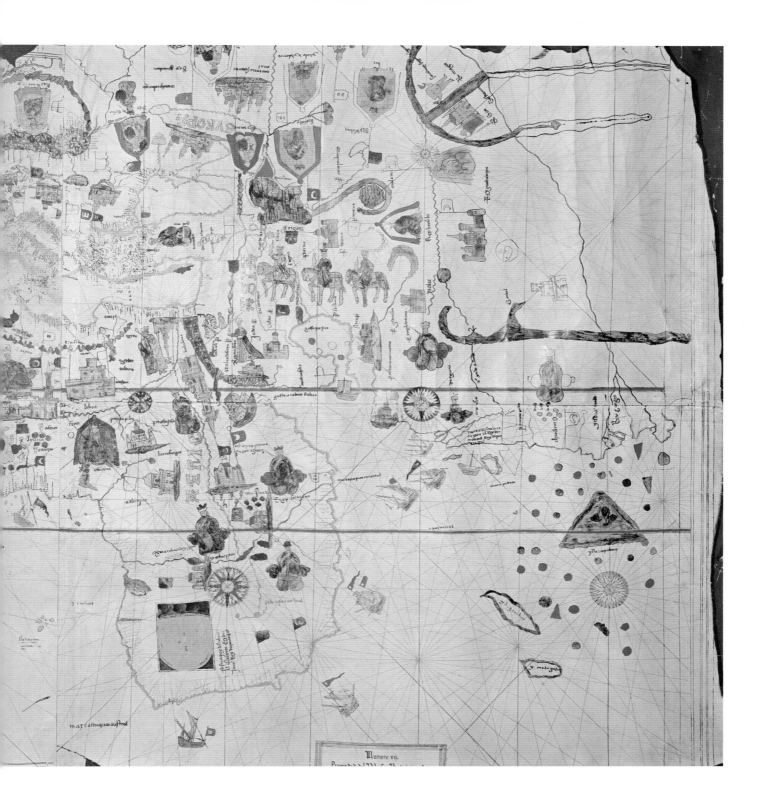

the New World map is larger than that of the Old World map. Consequently, the distance between Ireland and Newfoundland is artificially short, and locations in the New World do not line up accurately with those in the Old World. The join is along a meridian running through the Azores. The coast of the New World is shown curving around, with North America at the top and South America at the bottom. The island of Hispaniola is labelled.

WORLD MAP, JUAN VESPUCCI

This manuscript map, produced in 1503 by Amerigo Vespucci's nephew, Juan Vespucci, was probably either a draft or a copy of the *padron real* or *padron general* – the master map kept in Seville and on which all new discoveries were officially recorded. Vespucci sailed to the New World himself, and has marked on the map only locations and features of which he was personally certain. There are, consequently, areas of the interior left blank where his knowledge was lacking. The unknown parts of Asia are not covered at all, so removing the need to show the imagined coastline depicted on earlier maps.

CONTARINI–ROSSELLI MAP

The Contarini–Rosselli map was the first printed map to show the New World. Published in 1506, it reflects the belief of Columbus and his contemporaries that the newly discovered lands were part of Asia. The coniform map can be folded around to join the northern coastline opposite to the Asian landmass.

North America is not represented, except for some islands between Europe and Asia. South America is shown as a large mass of land that is not connected to any other, but continues off to the southwest, indicating terra incognita.

That the islands of Cuba and Hispaniola (now Haiti and the Dominican Republic) are shown in fairly close proximity to Japan, with no hint of a coastline above them, suggests Contarini did not know about Vespucci's voyage along the American coast in 1497. This is quite possible – new geographical information was often treated as a state secret while Spain and Portugal vied for dominance in the unexplored parts of the world.

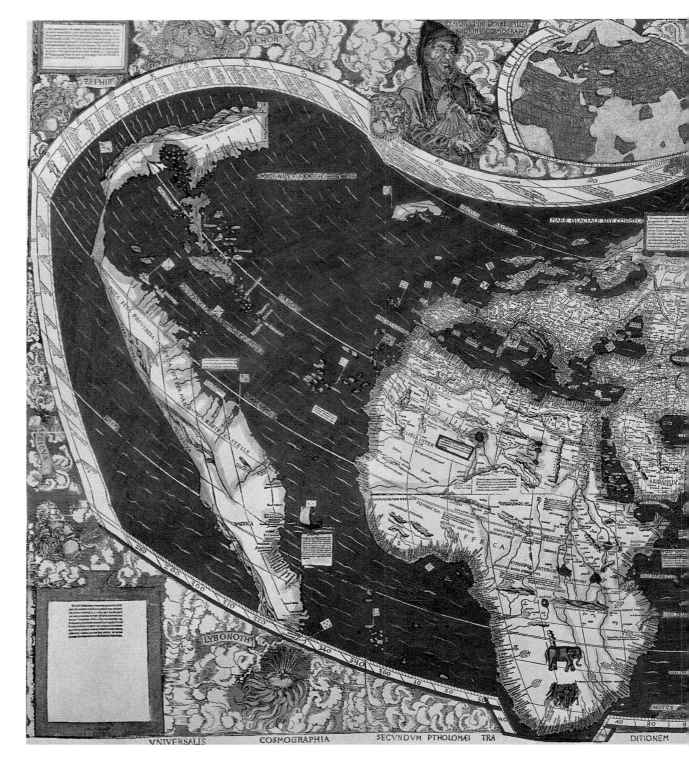

WORLD MAP, MARTIN WALDSEEMÜLLER

Martin Waldseemüller's Universalis Cosmographia, published in 1507, brings together the methods and aims of Ptolemy with the discoveries and tools of contemporary navigators. The map divides the world into eastern and western hemispheres, with Ptolemy illustrated over the east holding a quadrant and Amerigo Vespucci in the west holding a

compass. The map claims to be made in the tradition of Ptolemy and includes the discoveries of Vespucci and others. It is the first map to use the name 'America'.

The map includes the Pacific Ocean, which had not been discovered by Western navigators at the time. It has been suggested that Waldseemüller saw that the accounts of the New World were incompatible with descriptions of Asia and postulated there must be a sea between two continents. The 12 sheets of woodblock-printed map for wall-mounting were accompanied by paper gores for pasting onto a globe.

WORLD MAP, BATTISTA AGNESE

The map below, produced by Battista Agnese around 1542, appeared at the front of a world atlas he made at the request of the Holy Roman Emperor Charles V for his son (later Philip II). It correctly shows California as a peninsula, though later maps often represented it as an island. The route in black shows Magellan's circumnavigation of the globe in 1519–22, and that in gold shows the route from Spain through the isthmus of Panama to Peru, the source of a lot of Spanish gold.

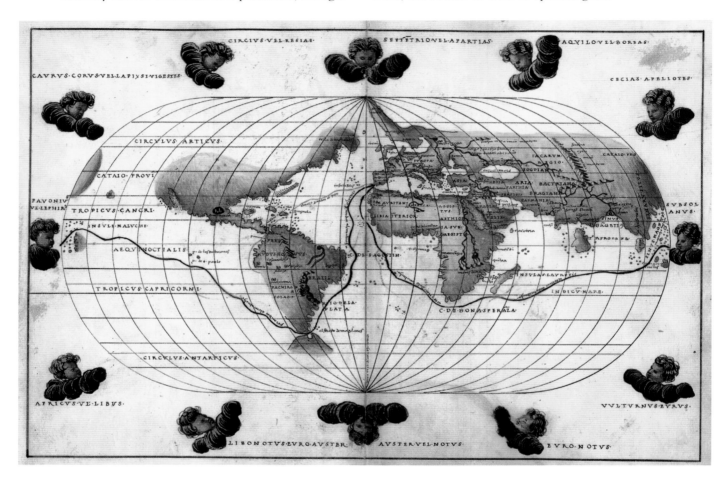

SOUTH AMERICA, PIRI REIS

This fragment of a map (facing page) produced by Piri Reis in 1513 shows the coastline of South America and the islands of the Caribbean on one side and North Africa and Spain on the other. Piri Reis claimed to have made it from 20 existing maps, including Christopher Columbus's own map, which has not survived. It is a portolan chart; Piri Reis also compiled a portolan atlas.

The map became more famous when claims emerged that it depicted parts of Antarctica, a continent not known at the time the map was made. The map shows the South American coastline bent round and continued (rather than a gap between Argentina and Antarctica), perhaps following the Ptolemaic theory that there was a large landmass in the south balancing those of the northern hemisphere. More fanciful interpretations have suggested that it is evidence of Chinese explorers having visited and mapped South America before Europeans arrived; that the map was copied from one created by a long-lost pre-Classical civilization, perhaps even mapping Antarctica before the current incursion of ice (in other words, more than 34 million years ago, long before the evolution of humans); or that Antarctica was mapped by aliens.

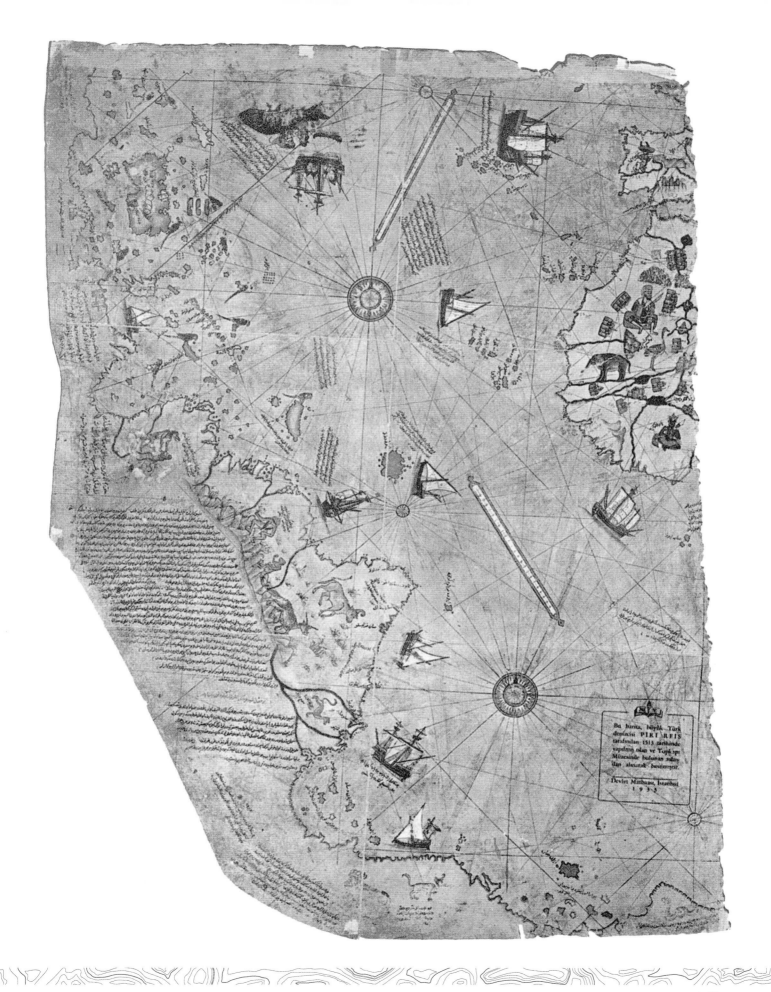

TYPUS ORBIS TERRARUM, ABRAHAM ORTELIUS

Abraham Ortelius's eight-leaved wall map of the world created in 1564 shows the vast projected continent of Terra Australis Incognita. This was the southern continent believed to balance the landmasses of the northern hemisphere, the 'Unknown Southern Land'. On this map, it is shown connected to Tierra del Fuego. The search for this land was a spur to exploration in the 16th and early 17th centuries. Gabriel de Castilla, who reported seeing snowy mountains beyond 64° S in 1603 might have been the first to sight Antarctica.

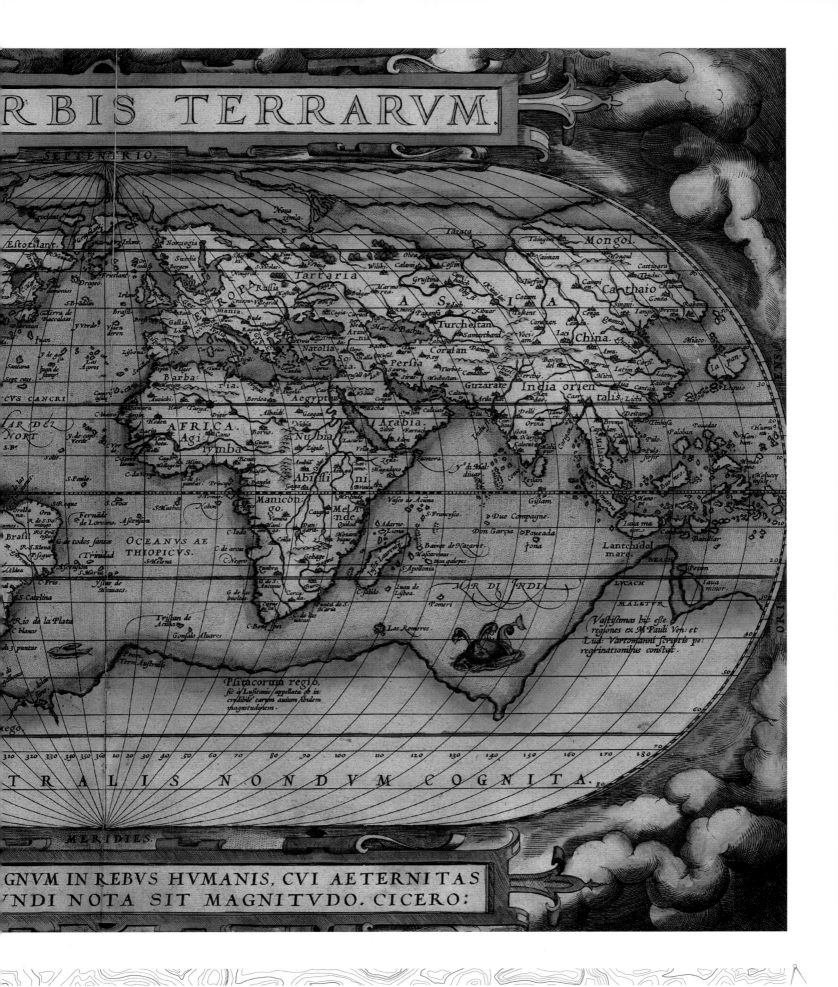

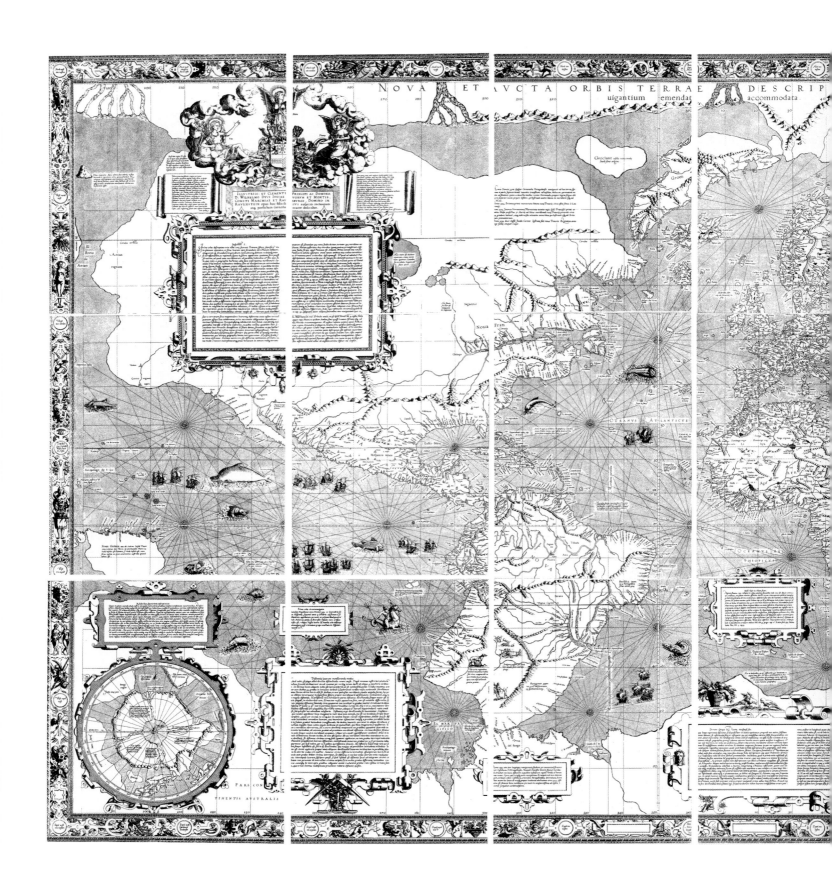

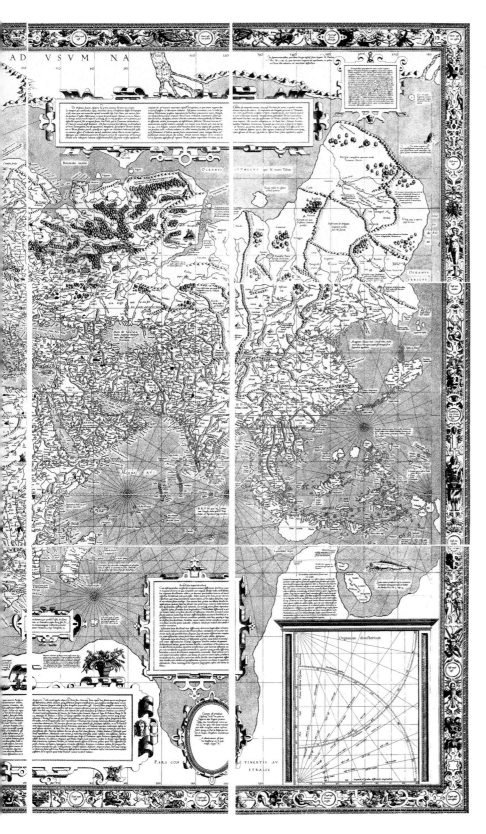

WORLD MAP, GERARDUS MERCATOR

Gerardus Mercator's world map, published in 1569, was revolutionary. It used a new projection – a way of depicting the spherical surface of the globe on a flat sheet – that he had developed specifically to aid navigation by sea.

The map is rectangular, with straight lines of longitude and latitude. The Mercator projection uses a variable scale, the same in horizontal and vertical directions at all points, but increasing as the latitude gets further from the equator. The disadvantage is that the scale becomes infinitely large at the poles, so it is not possible to depict the polar regions properly.

The distortion of land areas is extreme: Greenland appears the same size as Africa in the Mercator projection on modern maps, but in fact Africa is 14 times the area of Greenland. While the projection is ideally suited to navigation by sea, it came too early to be of practical use: the instruments necessary to make the measurements it relies upon were not available to ships' navigators until the mid-18th century, around 200 years later.

CALICUT, INDIA, CIVITATES ORBIS TERRARUM

Civitates Orbis Terrarum (see also pages 74–5) was the first city atlas, produced in six volumes by Georg Braun and Franz Hogenberg between 1572 and 1619. It contained 546 prospects, bird's-eye views and map views of cities around the world. More than 100 artists and engravers worked on the project altogether. The city plans and views were produced by different artists, some taken from existing work and modified as necessary. There is consequently no uniformity of style between maps of different regions.

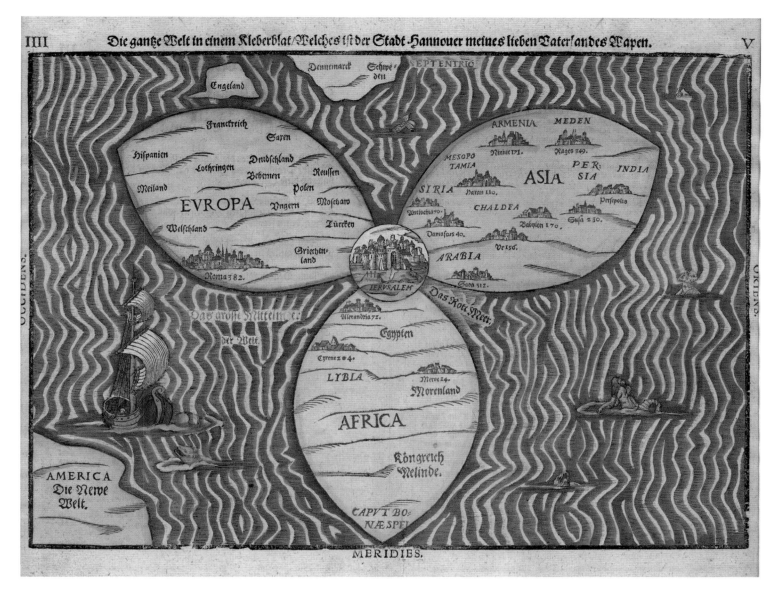

CLOVER LEAF MAP, HEINRICH BÜNTING

Another figurative map is the clover leaf map, a woodcut by Heinrich Bünting and included in his *Itinerarium Sacrae Scripturae* (*Travel Through Holy Scripture*), 1581. This book following the travels of biblical figures gives an account of the Holy Land, accompanied by geographical maps. The stylized map puts Jerusalem at the very centre of the world, following a common convention of mappae mundi, but inverts the tripartite form of the T-O maps, with Europe and Asia both at the top and only Africa at the bottom. The three-leafed clover arrangement might be intended to recall the Trinity of Christ, God the Father and the Holy Ghost. Cities and countries are illustrated and labelled within the continents. The places that don't fit lie outside the map, with England and Denmark off the coast of Europe and America creeping in from the lower left corner.

ATLAS MAJOR, JOAN BLAEU

Joan Blaeu was one of the greatest cartographers of the 17th century. His *Atlas Major*, published 1662–7, was a phenomenally ambitious undertaking, perhaps representing the pinnacle of the 17th century enthusiasm for atlases. Comprising 11 volumes in the first edition, it had 4,608 pages and 594 maps. Drawing a lot of his information from Dutch East India Company archives, Blaeu had access to everything he needed. He made the most of it – the *Atlas Major* was the largest book of the century. It was supposed to be the first in a three-part work, but the other two parts never appeared.

Blaeu shows much of the coast of North America, with a gap at the extreme northwest where the coast had not yet been mapped. He gives a partial outline of Australia, shows California as an island, and has an immense gap between eastern Russia and North America. The conjectural Antarctica is not present this time.

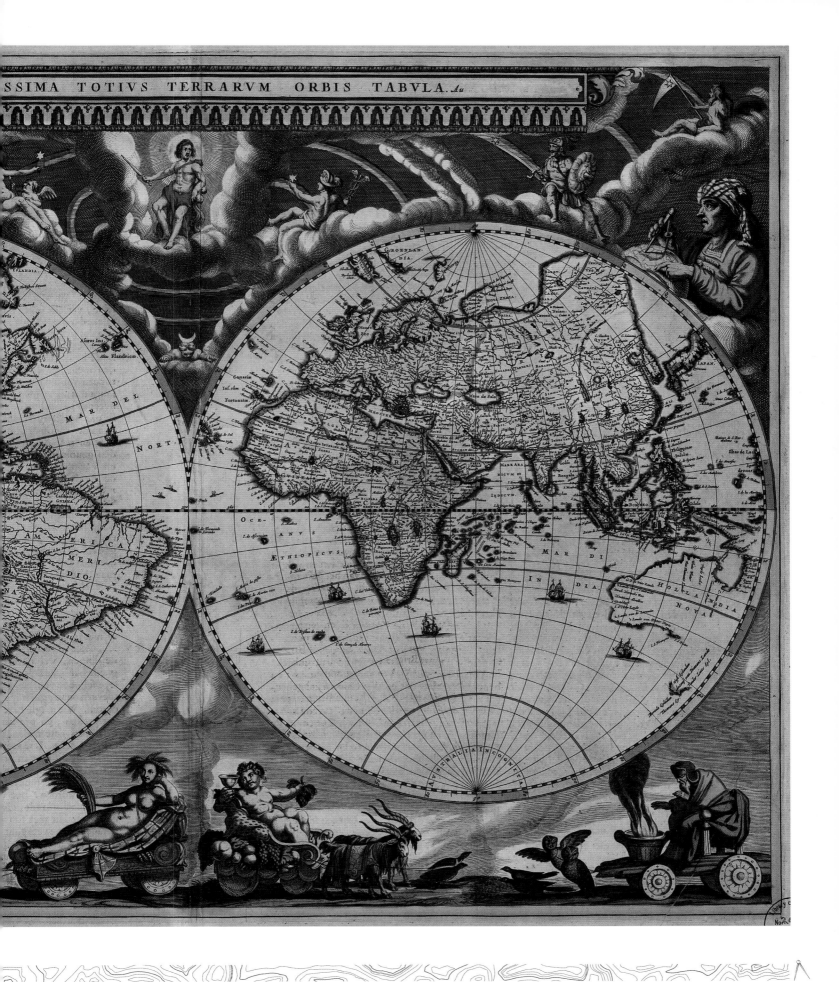

CH'ONHADO WORLD MAP

The Ch'onhado or 'All under heaven' maps were a traditional form of map drawn in Korea in the 17th, 18th and 19th centuries. The world is centred on China, Japan, Korea and the Ryukyus, surrounded by a ring of sea containing islands. There is an encircling continent and an exterior sea around that. The names of places in this sea are connected to descriptions of Taoist immortality. As the land forms get further from the centre, they are increasingly mythological and imprecisely depicted. India is on the left of the central continent; the Yellow River, the Yang-tse, and the Mekong are the rivers shown in this continent.

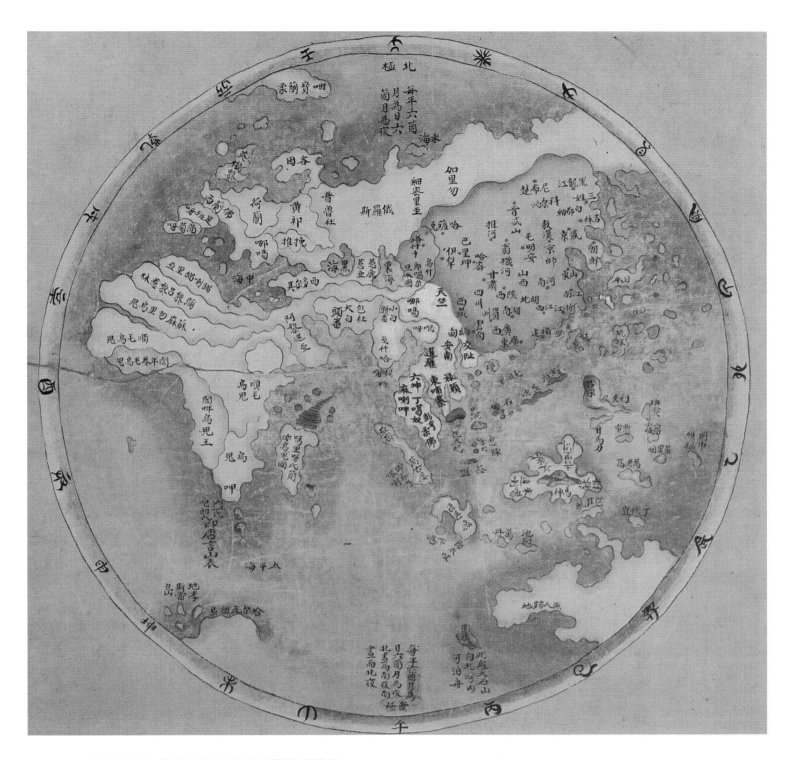

THE EASTERN HEMISPHERE

This map of the eastern hemisphere dates from 1790 and was made in China. It comes at the beginning of a scroll that is largely devoted to a coastal map. It relies on Western map-making traditions, yet omits the lines of latitude and longitude and provides the 24 Chinese points of the compass around the outside. This blending of Eastern and Western elements would have made the map unusable for purposes of navigation.

INTERNATIONAL MAP
OF THE WORLD

The International Map of the World was
a mapping project set up in 1913 under
which each country would produce its
own map of its territory according to
agreed standards. It was a grand plan:
there would be 2,500 maps covering the
whole world. Thirty-four nations agreed
to take part, creating maps to a scale
of 1:1,000,000 – they were sometimes
called the 'millionth maps'. Roads were
all to be in red, railways all in black,
and contours would be marked at
standard intervals in metres. World
War I threw a mighty spanner in the
works, though. By the mid-1920s Britain
and France had mapped 40 per cent of
the territories so far completed, and the
map had become a tool of imperialism.

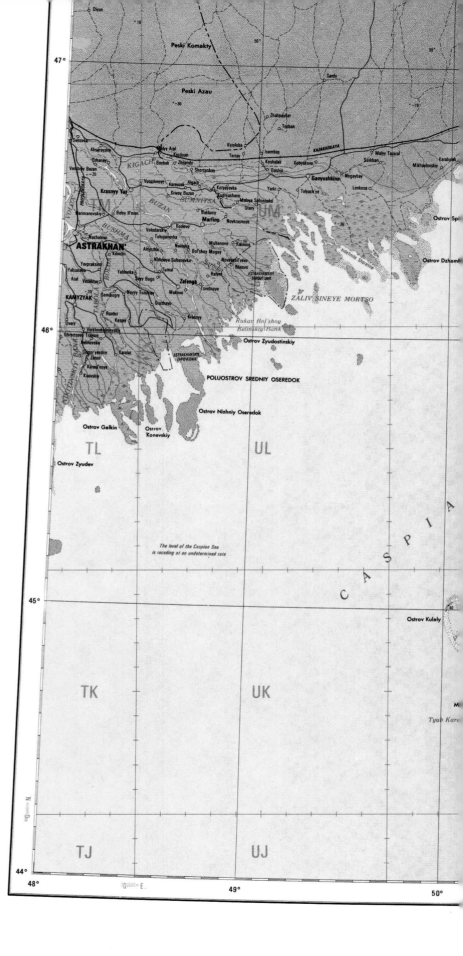

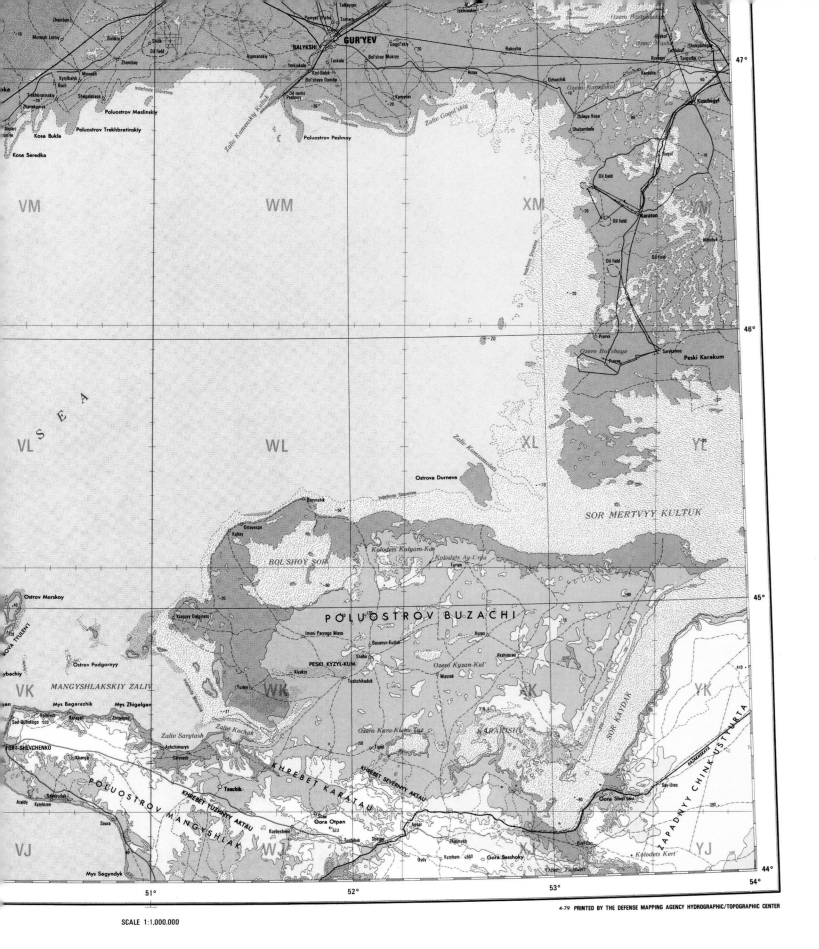

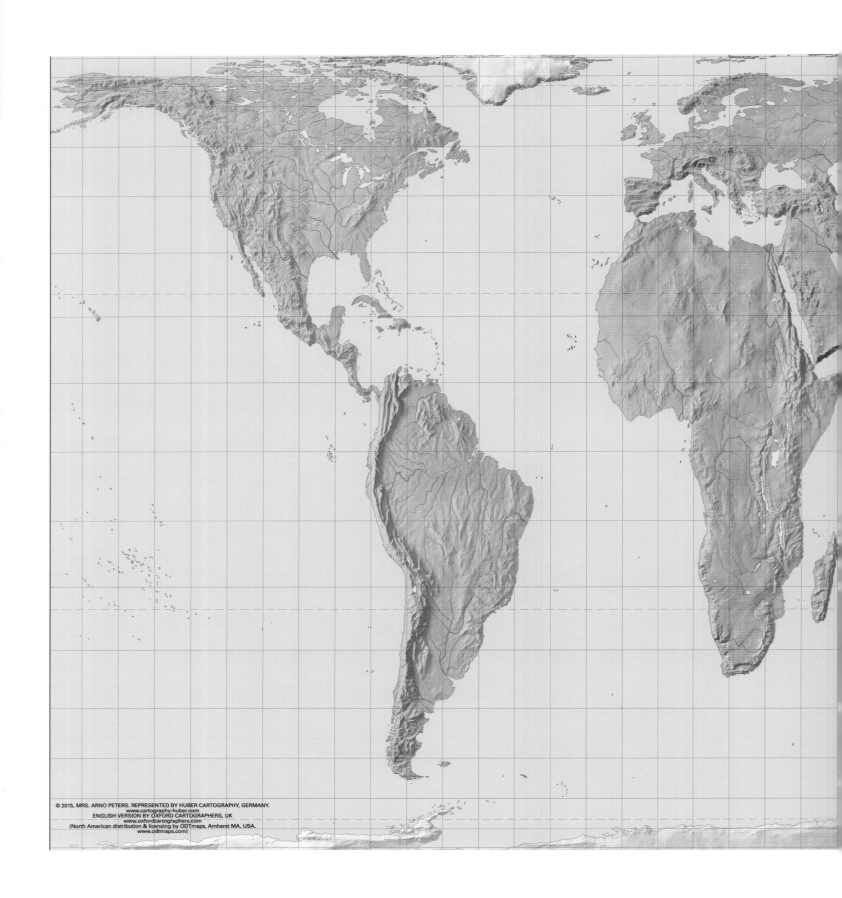

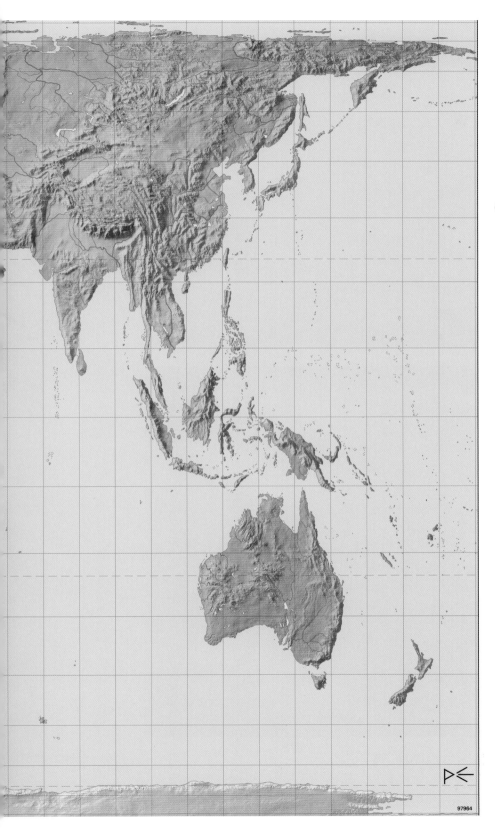

GALL–PETERS PROJECTION

Mercator's projection, which has been widely used since its development in 1569, distorts the size of the landmasses. Of particular political significance, it makes the countries of the northern hemisphere look much larger than they are compared to Africa. In 1855, James Gall introduced an alternative projection that makes the world look radically different. It is an area-accurate map, so ideal for comparing the areas of landmasses. Arno Peters developed it afresh and announced it as a new projection in 1974. It has some passionate advocates, and has been adopted by leading international organizations, including Oxfam and UNICEF.

GOOGLE EARTH

Google Earth is an interactive mapping project launched in 2005 that covers the whole surface of the Earth. A computer-based system, it allows users to zoom in on part of the world and see geographical features and buildings. The image is built up from satellite photos. Those of the USA are updated frequently, but many cities in other countries are represented by images collected in

2004. The surface can be viewed from an overhead or oblique perspective. Most land is shown to a resolution of at least 15 m (49 ft). Google Street View is integrated with Google Earth and can provide a view of a location as if the viewer were on the street there. Google Earth supports 'layers' with added data of any type. This sequence shows the effect of zooming in on Venice, Italy.

CHAPTER 5

THEME & USE

*Some maps focus on particular features
of an area or are drawn for a very specific use.*

THESE USES CAN VARY FROM AIDS to an activity, such as defence or escape, to recording and showing aspects of place-related information, such as geology or demographic data, to using a map to see emerging patterns in data. Understandably, uses of maps come once a culture is comfortable with mapping for its more usual functions of aiding travel, recording topography and detailing land ownership.

Some of the maps on the following pages, such as the octopus map on pages 180–1, assume an understanding of the geography the map depicts and build on that to make some kind of commentary. The outlines of major landmasses are now familiar to all of us, so we can interpret maps in quite sophisticated ways. Our ability to see the world from space, too, means that our view is no longer bound by the varied and inevitably distorting projections used to flatten the globe. We can see the world more truly, but also interpret it more freely than ever before.

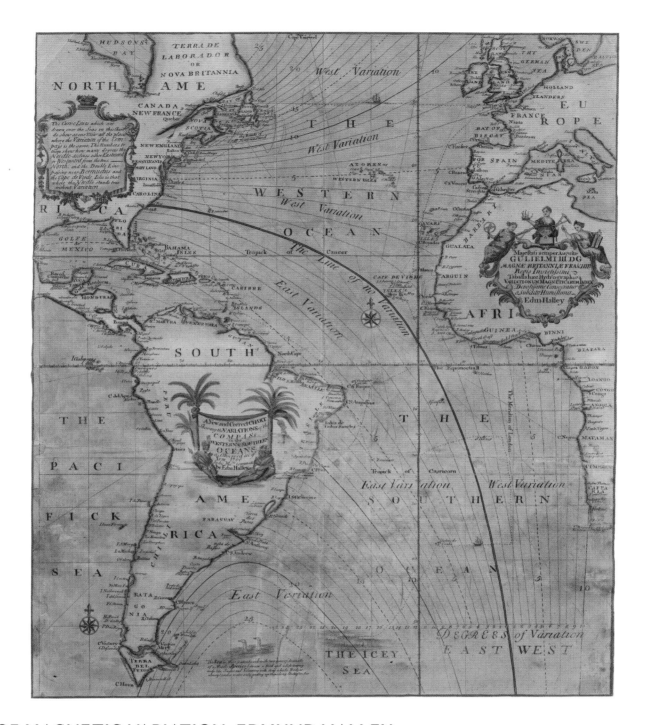

MAP OF MAGNETIC VARIATION, EDMUND HALLEY

Edmund Halley – more famous for his comet – drew this map in 1701. It shows the magnetic variation, or declination, of the Earth, and is called an isogonic chart. Magnetic variation is the difference between the geographic North Pole and the magnetic North Pole. Sailors had discovered that, as they moved around the globe, the compass did not always point to true or geographic north. The reason – that the Earth is a giant magnetic dipole – was discovered by William Gilbert in the late 16th century.

Halley thought he could solve the problem of measuring longitude if the magnetic variation was mapped. He was wrong – but his map is still used by physicists. Halley's method for making the map is not known, but he constructed it from data collected on two trips on *Paramore*, starting in 1698.

DELINEATION OF THE STRATA OF ENGLAND AND WALES, WILLIAM SMITH

William Smith drew the first map to show the geology of an entire country. He identified the layers of rock based on the type of fossils that could be found there rather than the geological composition of the rock itself. By doing this, he was able to judge the historic time period in which sedimentary rocks were laid down, and so began to move towards a true understanding of the age of the Earth, previously assumed in the West to be 6,000 years, following the account of the Bible.

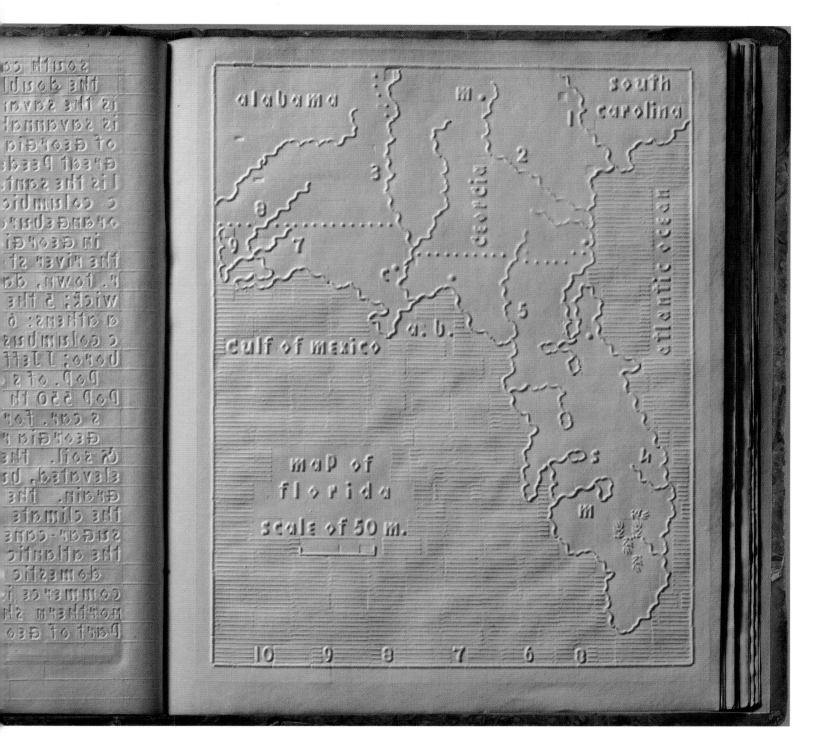

ATLAS FOR THE BLIND, SAMUEL HOWE

This atlas was designed by Samuel Howe in 1837 for use with pupils at the New England Institute for the Education of the Blind in Boston. It contains maps of 24 of the US states, with a page of text accompanying each. The maps are embossed on heavy paper, using conventions such as a fill pattern for water and series of short lines to denote mountains. The text is raised letters, not Braille, even though Braille had been invented 12 years previously.

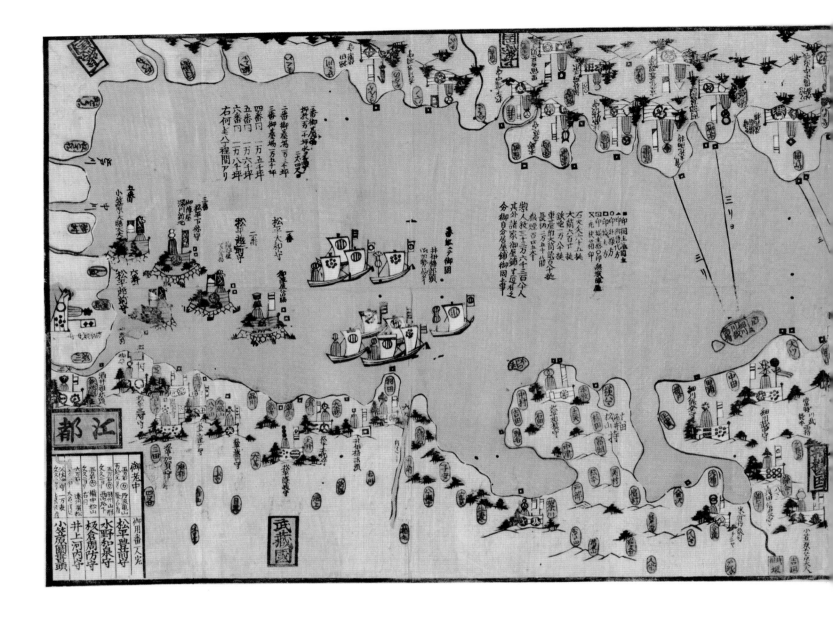

OKATAME MAP, TOKYO BAY

This coastal defence (*okatame*) map of Tokyo Bay, Japan, was prepared around 1860 as a response to a 'visit' in 1853 by Commodore Matthew C. Perry of the United States Navy with a fleet of warships. He entered the port of Yokohama near Edo (Tokyo), meeting no resistance. Although his stated objective was peaceful – to encourage Japan to trade with the outside world after two centuries of isolationist policy – the ruling shogunate saw the vulnerability of their seaboard.

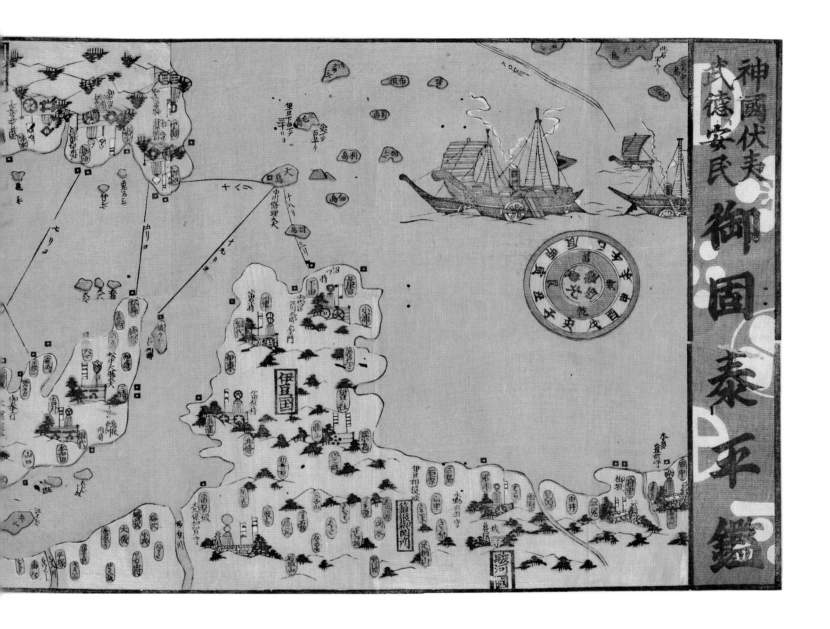

The map was prepared, with plans for 11 defensive forts along the coast in response to the perceived threat. Only five of the forts were ever built. North is at the lower left of the map, with Edo in the lower left corner.

The map is printed from a wood block, and is not to scale.

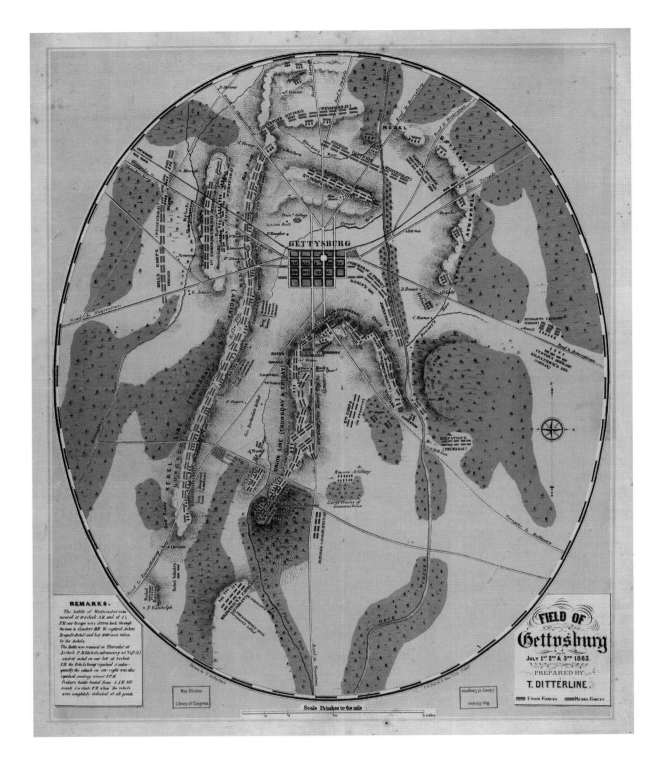

GETTYSBURG BATTLEFIELD, THEODORE DITTERLINE

This map of the battlefield at Gettysburg in 1863, drawn by Theodore Ditterline, shows the position and movement of troops and artillery, houses and the names of their residents, and aspects of terrain relevant to battle: slope, roads, railroads, tree cover and water courses. Relief is shown using hachures, an old alternative to contours. They are short strokes drawn in the direction of maximum slope. Steeper slopes are shown by shorter, thicker lines drawn close together; gentler slopes have a lower density of long, thin lines. Hachures are not numeric, so they give a good visual impression of slope, but are less useful than contours for scientific purposes.

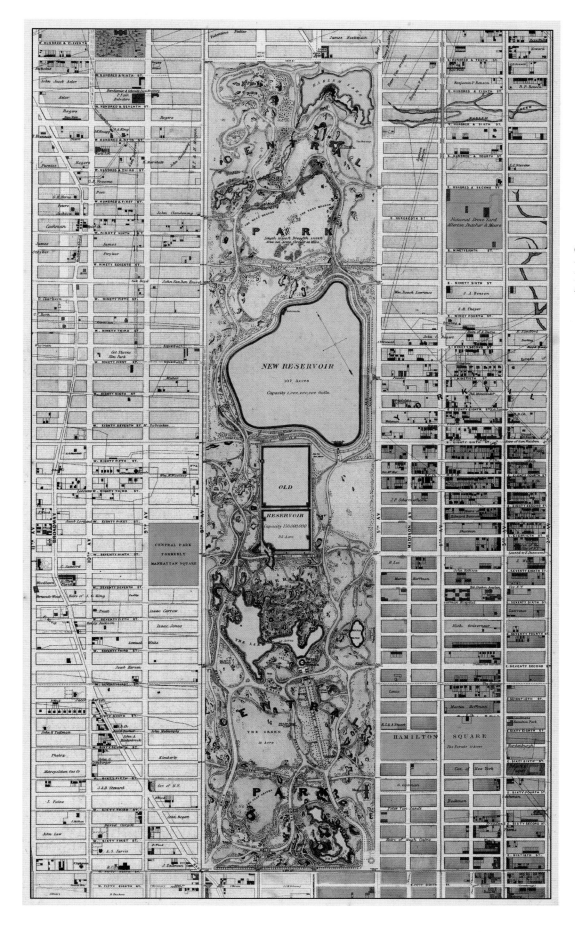

CENTRAL PARK, NEW YORK, MATTHEW DRIPPS

This map of Central Park on Manhattan Island, New York, was produced by Matthew Dripps in 1867, six years before the Park was officially opened. The final stages of construction and landscaping started in 1863, so Dripps' depiction is not far from the finished version. The contrast between the sinuous curves and natural shapes within the park and its enclosure in the city grid is particularly clear from the map. Orientation is approximately northeast, so that the lines of the streets are strictly vertical and horizontal.

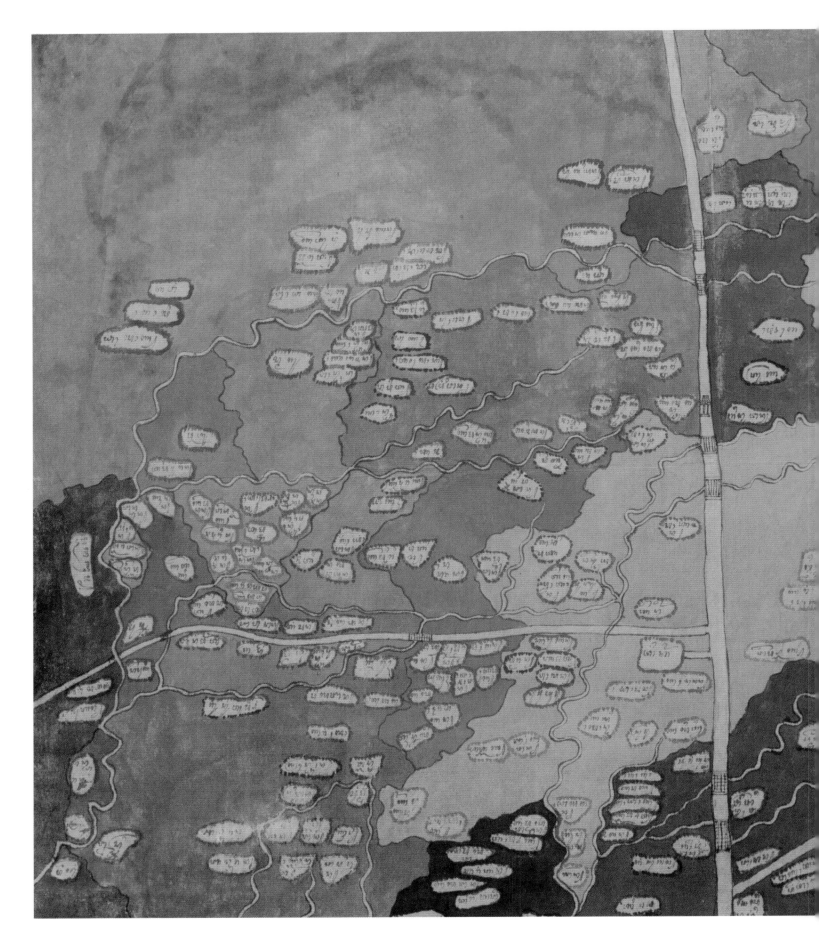

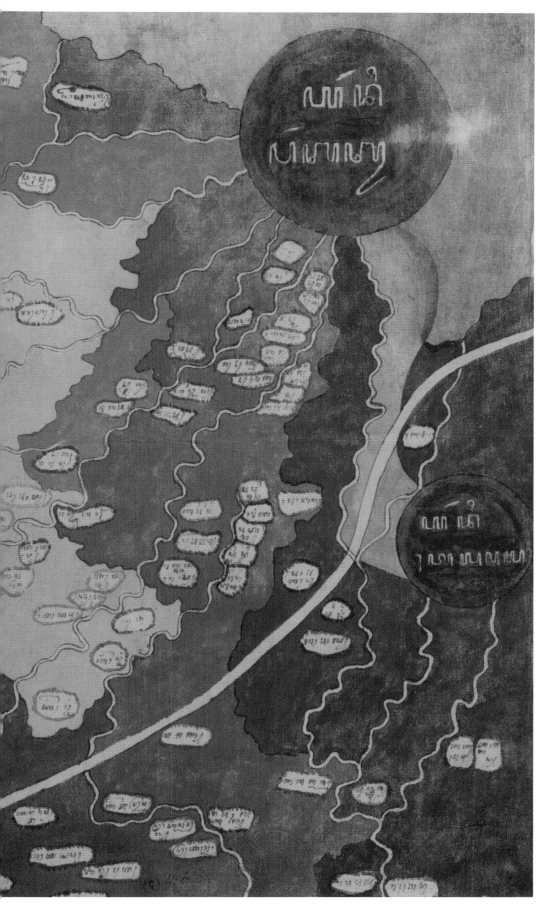

JAVA, ADMINISTRATIVE MAP

This administrative map of a small area in central Java was made in the mid-19th century, quite possibly for the Dutch authorities. It might have been used in collecting revenue from the settlements marked in the various colour-coded divisions. The two dark circles on the right are the volcanoes Merbabu (top) and Telomoyo. The summits of these two are 16 km (9 miles) apart, giving an idea of the scale of the map. South is at the top.

The colours go right to the edges of the map, suggesting that it might be one of a series which can be laid out together to show a larger area.

SERIO-COMIC WAR MAP, FRED ROSE

The cartographic octopus has its origins in the second half of the 19th century. It was used in a variety of maps to show how evil – a pernicious ideology or aggressive foreign power – sends its tentacles out into an area. There are octopus maps to show land-grabbing activities, greedy landlords, the rising power of dictators and, in one case, even a rapacious local council. Here, the Russian Empire is the octopus, extending its tentacles towards Europe. It already has Turkey, Persia and Poland in its grip.

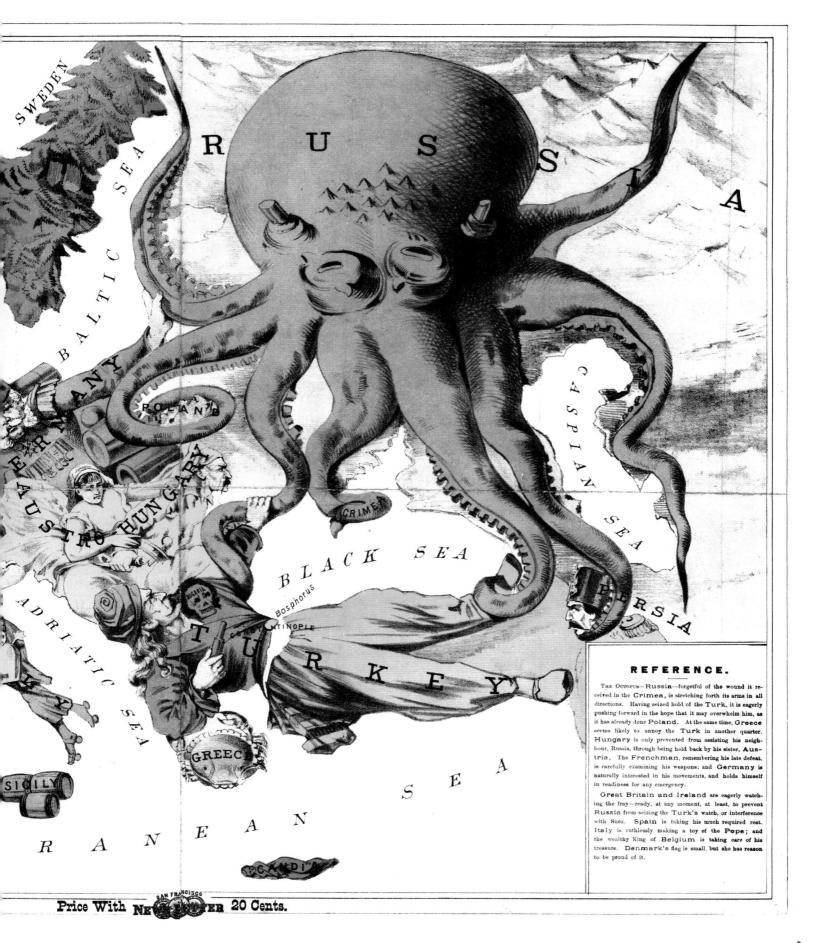

REFERENCE.

THE OCTOPUS—Russia—forgetful of the wound it received in the **Crimea**, is stretching forth its arms in all directions. Having seized hold of the **Turk**, it is eagerly pushing forward in the hope that it may overwhelm him, as it has already done **Poland**. At the same time, **Greece** seems likely to annoy the **Turk** in another quarter. **Hungary** is only prevented from assisting his neighbour, Russia, through being held back by his sister, **Austria**. The Frenchman, remembering his late defeat, is carefully examining his weapons; and **Germany** is naturally interested in his movements, and holds himself in readiness for any emergency.

Great Britain and Ireland are eagerly watching the fray—ready, at any moment, at least, to prevent **Russia** from seizing the **Turk's** watch, or interference with **Suez**. **Spain** is taking his much required rest. **Italy** is ruthlessly making a toy of the **Pope**; and the wealthy King of **Belgium** is taking care of his treasure. **Denmark's** flag is small, but she has reason to be proud of it.

Price With NEWSPAPER 20 Cents.

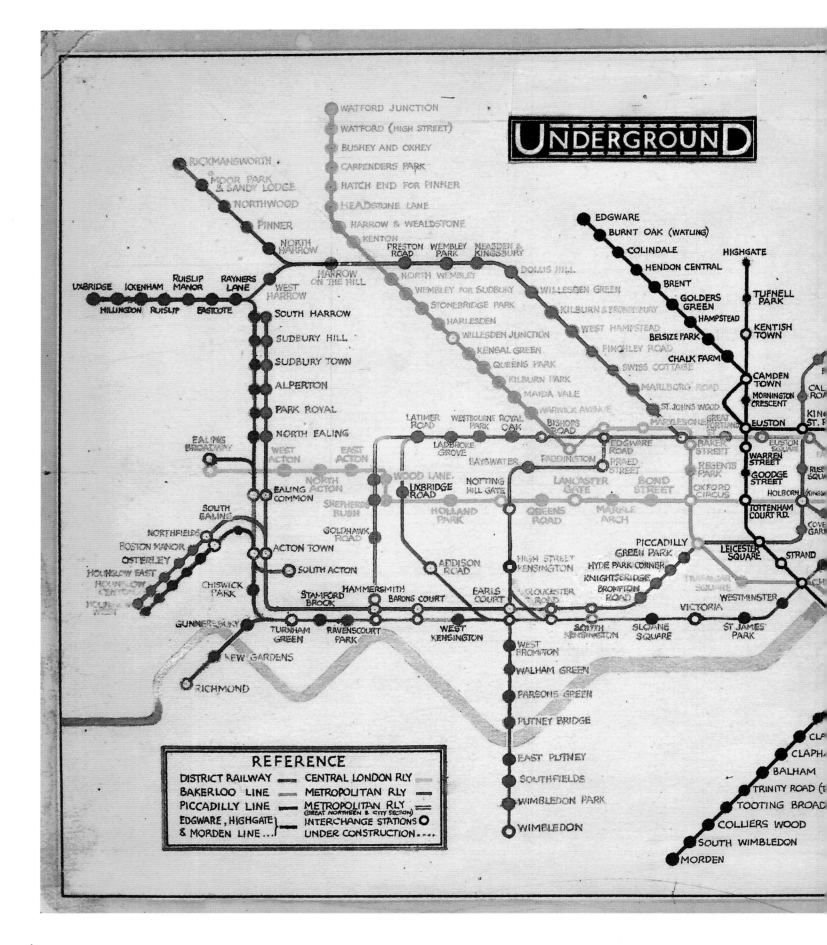

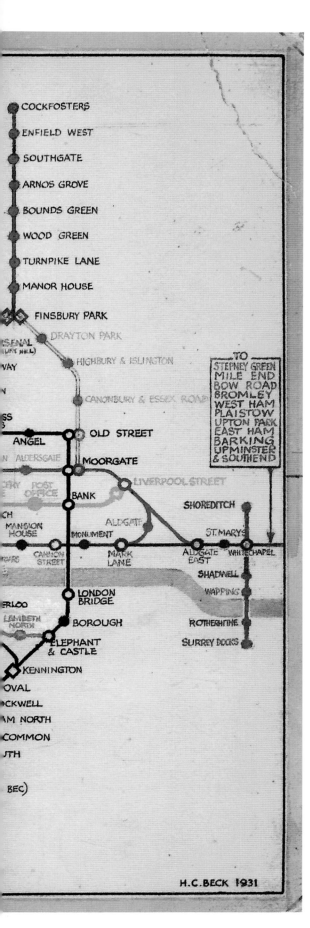

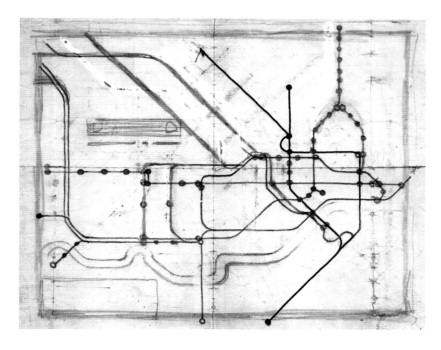

LONDON UNDERGROUND, HARRY BECK

The first version of the iconic topological map of the London Underground system was designed by Harry Beck in 1931 and published in 1933. It is a schematic diagram rather than a topographical map, showing the relative positions of stations and lines rather than their actual geographical locations. The map uses only straight horizontal and vertical lines, and diagonals at 45 degrees. Because distances are not shown to scale, even outlying stations can be included without overcrowding the dense central area. Interchange stations are represented by outline circles, and simple stations on a single line by solid circles. Beck began the map as a spare-time project while working for London Underground. It was adopted officially only after it became popular with the public when printed privately as a pamphlet. Above is an early preliminary sketch for the map by Beck.

MARSHALL ISLANDS, MATANG
(STICK MAPS)

Until the decline of inter-island
canoe travel in the 20th century,
Marshallese navigators detected
the proximity of islands still below
the horizon by the diffraction,
refraction and reflection of deep-
ocean swells. They made stick
charts to represent the changing
currents. These used bent and
straight sticks fastened onto a
reference grid. The navigator
had to look out for the 'knots'
(colliding crests) caused by swells
from different directions piling up.
The 'sticks' are the central ribs
of coconut leaves. Islands
are indicated by a shell tied
to the chart.

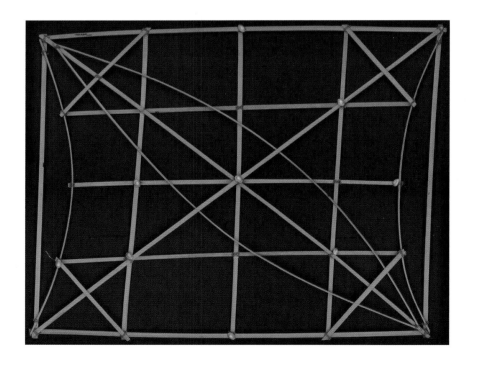

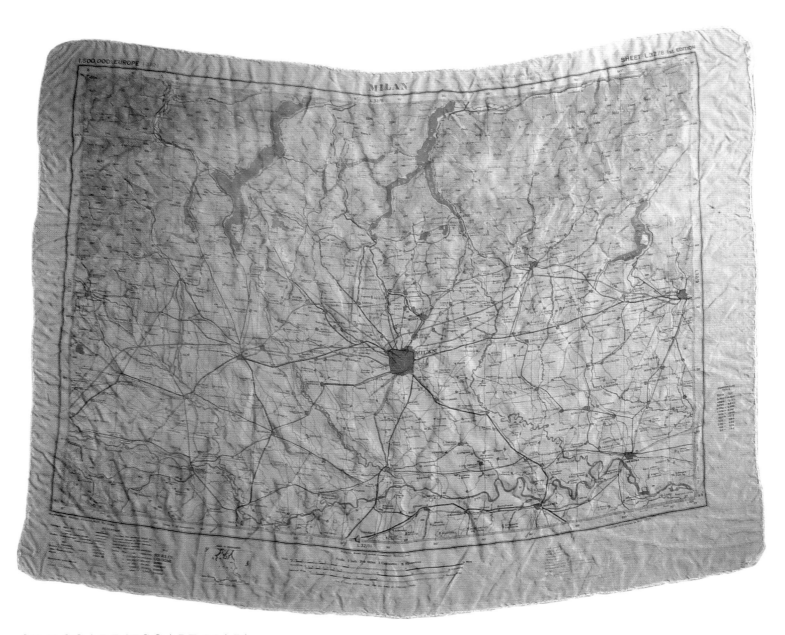

SILK SCARF 'ESCAPE MAP'

Escape maps have been used by pilots and others entering or crossing enemy territory during times of conflict. Printed on silk, they could be used as scarves and crushed into a very small space. They were light, durable and waterproof. Widely used by pilots in World War II, they helped those shot down to navigate enemy territory. More than 3.5 million silk and cloth escape maps were issued to Allied personnel during the war; this example, showing the area around Milan, was issued to Major Oliver Churchill.

ALLUVIAL VALLEY OF THE LOWER MISSISSIPPI RIVER, HAROLD FISK

This is one of a series of 15 maps which, when laid end-to-end, give a historical map of the length of the Mississippi river from southern Illinois to southern Louisana. The maps show how the path of the river has changed over time. The Mississippi is a sediment-rich river; periodically, sediment builds up in the current course until it switches to find a different channel. As part of a geological survey beginning in 1941, Fisk spent three years surveying over 2,000 miles of the river and its previous paths. Some of his map is conjectural, based on surviving physical evidence.

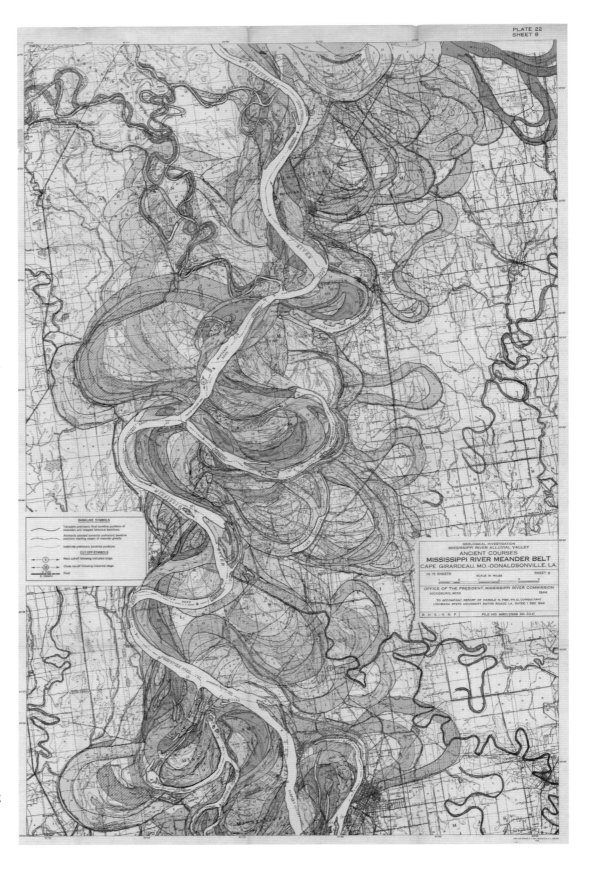

CHILD LABOUR

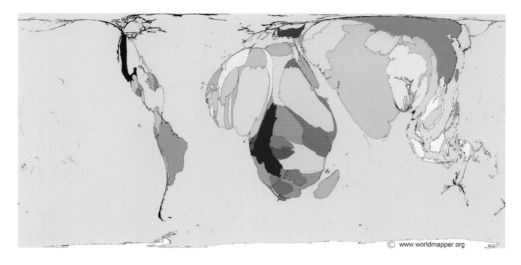

FEMALE ILLITERACY

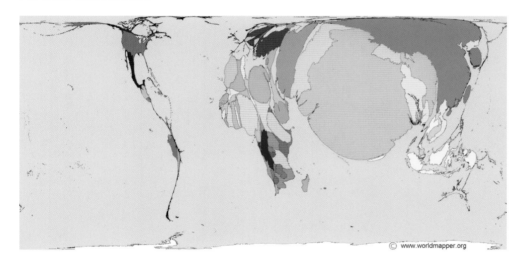

WORLD MAPPER PROJECT

The World Mapper project, started in 2005, redraws the countries of the globe at a size proportional to a dataset, usually relating to social geography. So, for example, if the size of countries is shown according to the personal wealth of the population, the USA is very large and Africa very small. It provides a vivid and immediate way of showing complex comparative data, using geography as a metaphorical approach.

PEOPLE LIVING ON $200+/DAY

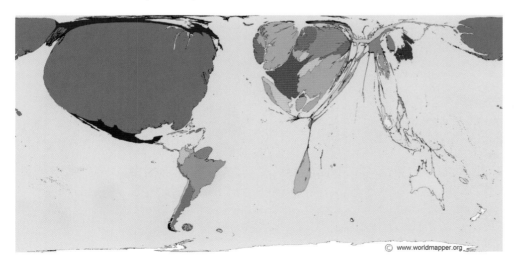

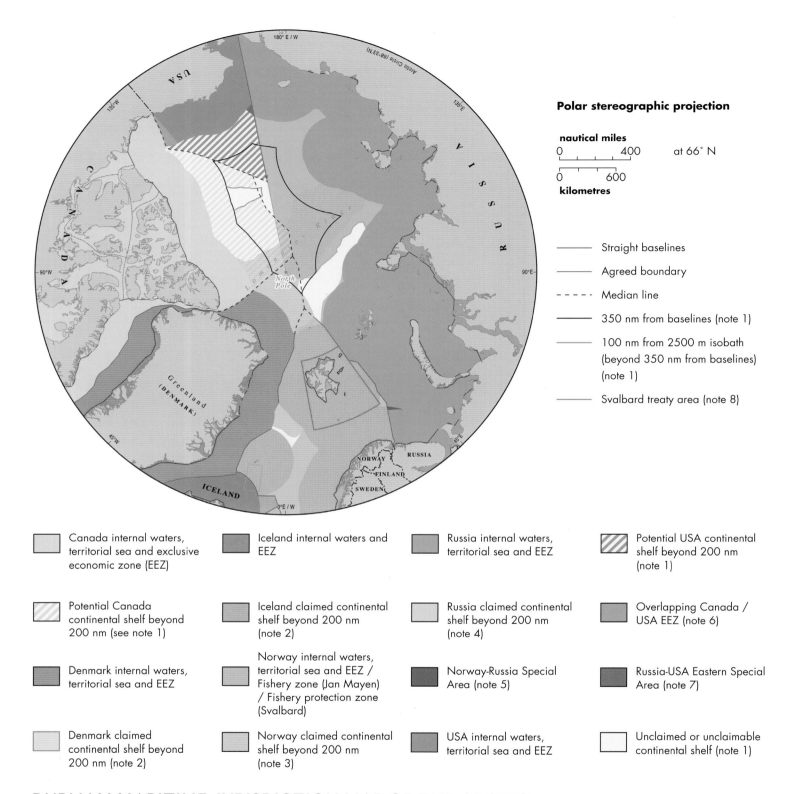

Polar stereographic projection

nautical miles

0   400   at 66° N

0   600

kilometres

———— Straight baselines

———— Agreed boundary

- - - - Median line

———— 350 nm from baselines (note 1)

———— 100 nm from 2500 m isobath (beyond 350 nm from baselines) (note 1)

———— Svalbard treaty area (note 8)

Canada internal waters, territorial sea and exclusive economic zone (EEZ)	Iceland internal waters and EEZ
Potential Canada continental shelf beyond 200 nm (see note 1)	Iceland claimed continental shelf beyond 200 nm (note 2)
Denmark internal waters, territorial sea and EEZ	Norway internal waters, territorial sea and EEZ / Fishery zone (Jan Mayen) / Fishery protection zone (Svalbard)
Denmark claimed continental shelf beyond 200 nm (note 2)	Norway claimed continental shelf beyond 200 nm (note 3)

Russia internal waters, territorial sea and EEZ	Potential USA continental shelf beyond 200 nm (note 1)
Russia claimed continental shelf beyond 200 nm (note 4)	Overlapping Canada / USA EEZ (note 6)
Norway-Russia Special Area (note 5)	Russia-USA Eastern Special Area (note 7)
USA internal waters, territorial sea and EEZ	Unclaimed or unclaimable continental shelf (note 1)

DURHAM MARITIME JURISDICTION MAP OF THE ARCTIC

As interest in resources under the Arctic ice-cap grows, disputes over which countries have the right to them will intensify. The IBRU Centre for Borders Research at the University of Durham has prepared a map that shows the current claims in the region, based on the rules set out by the United Nations Convention on the Law of the Sea in 1982.

The map shows known claims and agreed boundaries and indicates areas that might be claimed in the future.

LIGHT MAPS

Satellite photographs have given us new types of mapping images; these photos show landmasses at night-time, by their illumination. The density of light indicates urban development. The upper map shows North America, with the distinctive outline of the Florida coast (bottom right). The lower map shows Korea, with the southern half of the peninsula flooded with light and the northern half in darkness apart from a pinprick of light for Pyongyang, the capital of North Korea. China is lit up beyond the darkness.

FAULT-LINE AT PIQIANG, NASA

Satellite imagery can blur the line between maps and photographs. This image was taken using three different wavelengths of light and put together with false colouring to reveal the composition of the land. It shows the geological features of a fault-line in Piqiang, northwest China. When Smith mapped the strata of England and Wales (see page 172) he had to go to considerable trouble to determine the types of rock at each location. Where the rock is exposed, as here, the satellite image makes it relatively easy for geologists to identify the composition of the landscape and to see how the ridge has been split and offset by earthquake activity along the fault-line. Is it a map? Is the light image on the previous page a map? The definition of a map is not necessarily any clearer with modern images than with ancient ones.

INDEX